Music Has No Boundaries is a stor

It chronicles a valiant attempt t   lown artificial tribal walls. That takes sc   .pah. RAM FM was one-part people to ¡   .... across the lines and another part was flat out high voltage extreme octane rock and roll. Together they created a magic formula. That is probably why the RAM FM experiment with truth was stopped in its tracks by those who had a stake in the status quo. If anything, this story should leave you thinking what you can do to see everyone with the same degree of respect, appreciation, recognition, and acceptance as you wish to be treated with yourself.

—Dr Brian Polkinghorn
Department of Conflict Analysis and Dispute Resolution at
Salisbury University, and Fulbright Ambassador

Radio Nissa FM, the first and only women radio station in the Arab World, that I had the pleasure of visiting, is an incredible media platform that enlightens, inspires and empowers women.

—Rosanna Arquette, Hollywood actress / producer / director
Womanity Ambassador

Having followed the start-ups of RAM FM 93.6 and Nissa FM and being an avid fan of both, I knew bits and pieces of their stories. This insider account brings the entire picture into full color, weaving the bold story of two radio stations with the myriad of complications of a region fraught with turmoil. If I didn't know better, I would say this had to be fiction, but sadly it's a true story, one I still live in today.

—Sam Bahour, Palestinian-American Business Consultant
Originally from Youngstown, Ohio, now
based in Al-Bireh / Ramallah

I just finished reading *Music Has No Boundaries*. I was riveted. It's a great tale of perseverance. I'm delighted that RAM FM will survive for posterity in this worthy book, and will outlive the broadcast of that last tearful goodbye.

—Nicholas Pelham, *The Economist*,
Middle East Correspondent, London

MUSIC HAS NO BOUNDARIES

Bob Marley and the Beatles + Call-in Radio = A Bridge Over Troubled Waters in Israel/Palestine

RAFIQUE GANGAT

 Cune

Dedicated to my son Adam

Music Has No Boundaries:
Bob Marley, the Beatles + Call-in Radio =
Bridge Over Troubled Waters for Israel / Palestine
by Rafique Gangat
© 2022 Rafique Gangat Cune Press, Seattle 2022
First Edition

Paperback	ISBN 9781951082178
Hardback	ISBN 9781951082475
EPUB	ISBN 9781614574194
Kindle	ISBN 9781614573470

Library of Congress Cataloging-in-Publication Data

Names: Gangat, Rafique, author.
Title: Music has no boundaries : Bob Marley, the Beatles + Call-in Radio =
Bridge Over Troubled Waters for Israel / Palestine
/ Rafique Gangat.
Description: First edition. | Seattle : Cune Press, [2022] | Includes
index. | Summary: "93.6 RAM FM, a pioneering English radio station in Palestine/Israel"
-- Provided by publisher.
Identifiers: LCCN 2020013355 | ISBN 9781951082178 (paperback) | ISBN
9781614573470 (kindle edition)
Subjects: LCSH: FM broadcasting--Israel--History. | Radio
broadcasting--Israel--History. | FM broadcasting--West Bank--History. |
Women in radio broadcasting--West Bank--History. | Radio and women--West
Bank--History.
Classification: LCC HE8699.I75 G36 2020 | DDC 384.5406/55694--dc23
LC record available at https://lccn.loc.gov/2020013355
330 p 04-24-2022 SCD

Bridge Between the Cultures (a series from Cune Press)

Afghanistan & Beyond	Linda Sartor
Congo Prophet	Frederic Hunter
Confessions of a Knight Errant	Gretchen McCullough
Empower a Refugee	Patricia Martin Holt
Nietzsche Awakens!	Farid Younes
Stories My Father Told Me	Helen Zughaib, Elia Zughaib
Apartheid is a Crime	Mats Svensson
Arab Boy Delivered	Paul Aziz Zarou

Syria Crossroads (a series from Cune Press)

The Dusk Visitor	Musa Al-Halool
White Carnations	MusaRahum Abbas
East of the Grand Umayyad	Sami Moubayed
The Road from Damascus	Scott C. Davis
A Pen of Damascus Steel	Ali Ferzat
Jinwar and Other Stories	Alex Poppe

Cune Cune Press: www.cunepress.com | www.cunepress.net

Contents

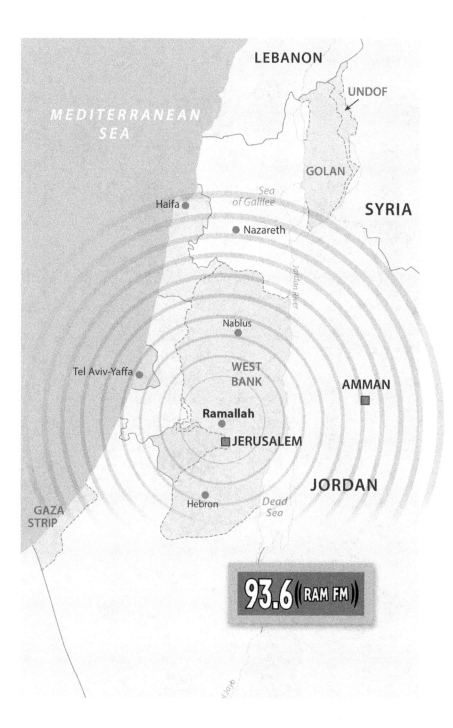

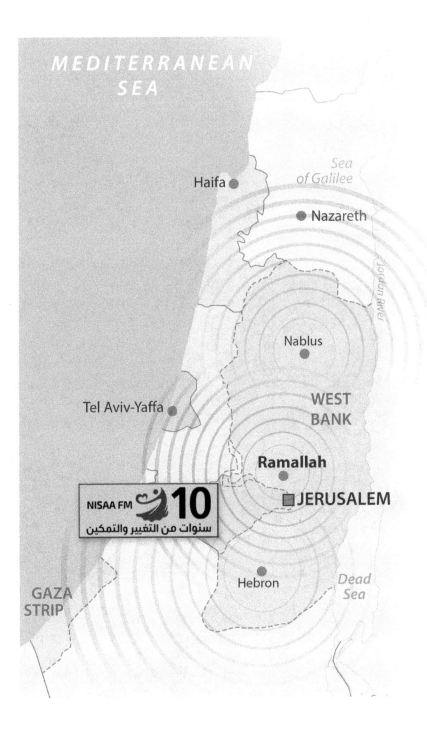

1 The Beginning

Inspired by the lessons of the South African experience

JOHANNESBURG, SANDTON: June 28, 2005—it was Radio 702's twenty-fifth anniversary.

Primedia hosted a huge party on their premises. It was a celebration of the role Radio 702 had played in building bridges amongst the racially segregated and divided peoples of South Africa, followed by the reconciliation of the nation—all from its humble beginnings as a rock 'n' roll station to its progression to an all-talk format station.

The who's who in government and media was there, and it was truly a wonderful celebration. Nelson Mandela could not attend in person but he did so in spirit, with a touchingly recorded message, that the entire audience felt in their hearts. Mandela congratulated Radio 702 for the role it had played during apartheid and continued to do in reconciliation and nation building.

I was not only inspired by the occasion but energized that we could do the same in Palestine and Israel, where we were busy trying to set-up a similar type of radio station and build a bridge between warring Semitic cousins.

And this is how that all began—I was the South African Representative to the Palestinian Authority, in a sense, the Ambassador, and I received a phone call from an acquaintance, Yusuf Abramjee, who said, "Hello Rafique, deputy minister Aziz Pahad referred me to you to assist us. My chairman, Issie Kirsh, is here with me and he wants to talk to you." His boss was listening to the conversation on the speakerphone and interjected, "Good morning, I am Issie. Can I call you Rafique?" To which I responded, "Yes! Please do."

"Rafique, I am coming to Tel Aviv," he said. "I will be staying at the Hilton Hotel. Can we meet over lunch in two days' time to discuss an important matter with you?"

On 8 July 2003, I made my way to Tel Aviv, not having the faintest idea why Issie Kirsh, chairman of Primedia, wished to meet me. All I knew was how he had pioneered South Africa's first-ever Indian radio station, Radio Truro from Swaziland in the 1980s, on a weak medium wave signal for the million plus Indians in South Africa. With all its limitations, it was an enormous success for a community deprived of music in apartheid South Africa and when that was shut down, he had launched Radio 702. The 702 studios were in Johannesburg, but he had obtained a license in Bophuthatswana

9

Issie Kirsh

(Apartheid homeland) based the transmitter there and made the connection via a telephone link. This was an ingenious way of circumventing the barriers put in place by the apartheid regime, designed to block independent media. Those who persevered had regularly been in the firing line of the president at the time, PW Botha, who had often summoned Issie to castigate him. Issie had gained not just notoriety but also the respect of the victims of apartheid for his principled stance. This happened when Radio 702 transformed from being a rock 'n' roll station to "talk" and took on issues that the state media brushed under the carpet. Issie had grown into a media tycoon with the acquisition of three more radio stations in the country.

As a former music impresario and radio personality, prior to becoming a diplomat, I reminisced on my own musical journey, on my way to Tel Aviv.

I grew up in apartheid South Africa—we were separated, according to race and color—Black/White/Asian, and Colored—and we lived segregated lives, with legally enforced boundaries.

LM Radio, which broadcast from the neighboring country of Mozambique, provided us a diet of pop and rock music, which was anathema to the apartheid regime, that dished out conservative music to whites and ethnic music to the other races, in order to maintain the boundaries amongst us.

But the apartheid regime was powerless—music has no legally enforced boundaries, sound waves flow, as far as they are broadcast, cutting across both physical and intellectual limits.

LM Radio obtained a cross-section of Black/White/Colored and Asian listeners, as it freed up our perceptual horizons, taking us beyond the boundaries of South Africa, into Africa and a world beyond.

Whenever, and the occasions were indeed rare, I met with fellow South Africans, especially white South Africans, our common musical tastes created a bridge on which to reach out, communicate and bond with.

Once, traveling from Cape Town, on the scenic garden route, I helped two white women whose car had broken down by giving them a ride to the next town. On the way, they listened to my selection of music and marveled that it was what they listened to as well. It led to the beginning of a friendship that lasted many years.

Fast forward: In 1979, I enrolled at a Whites-only university, by virtue of special permission from the Minister of Police, as I sought to study, the African language, Zulu, which was not offered as a course by my Asian university. We were a handful of non-white students in a vast ocean of whites, and for me, I quickly found in music, the ties that bind, and many wonderful and meaningful friendships were forged.

Betus was a university rock band made up of a number of my friends—Philip Mitchell, who hailed from Scotland, Chris Massey, from Benoni, Graeme Gilfillan, a local lad, and Andrew Gwillam, from Durban. They were a motley crew, bound by a common desire to play original music—influenced by rock but essentially home grown.

The first time I heard them play, I was impressed by their talent and immediately became their manager. Jointly, we charted a course through our final year at university. We bought sound equipment on an installment basis and then had to find gigs so we could make the payments.

This was a period in South Africa when the white nightclubs played recorded music and occasionally accommodated bands that played cover versions of popular songs. The Indian-Colored nightclubs were influenced by African-American music, and the black clubs played traditional music in a variety of local languages. So, in terms of the market, a white rock band that played original, never-before-heard music, was a rarity and we had to create a new audience altogether.

Our journey that year took us through many unusual venues, from a supper club for Indian families at a hotel in Pietermaritzburg, my university town, to a bar for black workers at a hotel in nearby, Richmond. Somehow, we made the monthly payments on the sound equipment and the band progressed very nicely. By the end of the year, we were confident enough to take a shot at the Battle of the Bands contest and made our way to Johannesburg to showcase the Betus talent to record company executives.

A weekend before the contest we had a visit from our friend Gary, who had dropped out of university to work on a coalmine in the town of Glencoe, between Pietermaritzburg and Johannesburg. Gary was impressed with the band and set about to arrange a gig. He said he would personally make the necessary arrangements with the mine management. He was sure it would go down well because there was generally no entertainment for the miners on weekends.

On our way to Johannesburg, we drove to a hall at the center of the coal mining compound that was to be our venue for the show that evening. When we started carrying the equipment inside we had many eager, curious helpers and it didn't take us long to set up everything on the stage.

Then the wait began for the anticipated crowds to appear.

The charge for the show was a meager amount, given the crowd we were anticipating, we expected to cover our fuel costs for the trip. However, the experience and being able to use the gig as a warm-up before we reached Johannesburg were far more important to all of us.

As time went by, we started getting worried because only a trickle of onlookers had arrived and waited outside. Then no more came. The rest remained in the hostels, presumably doing whatever they normally did on a Saturday night.

But we were hoping to make it an out-of-the-ordinary Saturday night; one they would remember for a long time. Concerned, I asked, "Gary, did you advertise the gig?" "Yes, we did!" Then, one of the miners approached me and we began to make small talk. He was surprised to learn that I was the boss of the white boys. Just as he said, "Tell these boys to play some music, so I can hear," the band began to do a sound check, which they performed with great passion.

My new friend's eyes lit up; he loved the sound he was hearing. It was a mixture of rock and reggae, with lots of African influences—a truly South African sound.

He grabbed a megaphone and went running around the hostel compound, inviting everyone to come and see,. "Look!" he shouted, "White boys making music and jumping like monkeys." Miners rolled out of their hostels and headed to the hall, which was soon packed to capacity, and the band churned out song after song, with no respite.

Our audience jived the night away, enjoying themselves to the max. Seeing four white boys entertaining a crowd of black coalminers in their compound during the days of apartheid was somehow a calling for me.

That was when I realized the power of music: it has no boundaries. It's a universal language that transcends race, class and color divides, uniting all.

The gig ended in the early hours of Sunday morning when the guys, fueled until then by audience enthusiasm, reached a peak of exhaustion and simply couldn't continue anymore. The drunk, exhausted, and fully satisfied miners helped load up the equipment and escorted the cars all the way out of the mine, calling out their thanks as we crawled along to the exit.

That this white band had lit up at least one Saturday night for these miners was special.

We then made it to Johannesburg, but before we could even take part in the Battle of the Bands contest, tragedy struck. Chris and Andrew heard that the army had called them up to do border duty. On principle, they refused to go and immediately headed to London.

I remained in Johannesburg to partner with Dirk Ackerman, Karl Windrich and Anthony Fisher in Progressive Productions, an entertainment production company based in Troye Street, Hillbrow. We were committed to South African music, staging concerts, recording local music, and marketing and promoting the artists and their indigenous work. Our goal was to establish a significant local industry and not to remain slaves to the general fare of American music.

This was my chosen career and I was highly motivated. It was the most logical move from the experiment I had initiated in my university laboratory with Betus. The personal motivation that fueled my passion was: music has no racial boundaries and it ought to play a meaningful role in bringing people together.

One morning, I had a call from the head of the student council at Rand Afrikaans University (now the University of Johannesburg). He was looking for a music group to play at an event on campus that evening. I gave him the names of the groups we had on our books who were available. When I got to Dennis East and Stingray, a pop-rock outfit, the caller said, "Yes, we'll take them." He readily accepted the contract and terms of payment and the gig was on.

Progressive Productions was staging three concerts that evening and my good friend and colleague, Ruth, accompanied me to all the venues to see whether all our productions were running smoothly.

First stop was the Great Hall at the liberal Wits University, where the Malopoets, a Black band was dishing up an exciting African-jazz fusion fare. The audience was largely made up of English liberals and hippie-type academics that all applauded the music—although the leader of the band later confessed that they'd been out of tune because they'd had problems with the sound system and acoustics. Nevertheless, white liberals patronized and applauded them, giving their bleeding hearts a sense of satisfaction. Most importantly, the Malopoets group was well paid, and the audience was entertained.

Next stop was the white Rand Afrikaans University, to check out the gig I had arranged earlier in the day. It was the first time I had set foot on an Afrikaner campus, and I immediately felt intimidated by the configuration of the buildings. They were arranged in a laager reminiscent of the circle of wagons Afrikaners formed during their frontier days. For me, it symbolized their closed-minded attitude. But I was in for a bigger surprise when Ruth and I reached the concert venue. Students were dressed formally—the men wearing black suits, white shirts and black ties and the women wearing ball gowns.

Partners were weaving around the dance floor, leading arms outstretched, in the typical Afrikaner ballroom style.

Ruth and I found this hilarious. To be fair though, the dancers were having a good time. Dennis and his band didn't mind because the financial reward was good, and I questioned how fair it was of me to judge a different culture.

Last stop was the Selbourne Hall in downtown Johannesburg where the Asylum Kids and Springbok Nude Girls, two hard rock bands, were playing. The venue was packed to capacity with white kids dressed in biker and rock attire, mostly drunk or high on drugs. The music was extremely loud and everyone was having a real blast; some were even hanging from the curtains.

In the early hours of the morning, Ruth and I sat down and, over coffee, I said, "What a night; three white audiences enjoying different types of music in one city. What amazing diversity we have, and the possibilities are endless. If we can only harness all this properly we can be a world leader in music."

Ruth agreed, "All the ingredients are there, they just need to be put together."

And we then talked about similar experiences on the black side of town on other nights. Coloreds were really into disco music, as were Indians. But in the black areas, traditional compositions in the various local languages dominated, with the influence of reggae and its protest message creeping in. As rock music was apparently seen as "white man's music," it was abhorred. Apartheid had unintentionally created rich diversity, but it was being wasted due to division and prejudice. It took Paul Simon to pull it all together a few years later, in 1986, when he collaborated with, among others, Ladysmith Black Mambazo, Ray Phiri and Stimela for his international hit album Graceland.

Why we could not do it on our own has always intrigued me, but at least I can't be accused of not trying.

Plumb Crazy was a whites-only nightclub in Hillbrow, a suburb of Johannesburg, during the early eighties. It played mainly disco music and often staged local bands doing cover versions of the current hits. One night, the white band that was scheduled to play canceled and all I had to offer the desperate manager was an excellent colored band named Wayne & Vic. After much persuasion, and resistance, it was finally agreed that they would play. It was a chance we were all going to take because we were aware that the club would be violating the Group Areas Act and the Liquor Laws—key apartheid era laws.

That night, Wayne & Vic had the crowd screaming for more and the duo obliged by playing way past midnight.

This meant they missed their train to the colored township of Reiger Park, which was on the other side of town. So I took them to my apartment in downtown Johannesburg, which was in a white area. The Indian caretaker, Fakir Moola, accommodated other Indians quietly and discreetly at exorbitant rentals. But it suited me to live in the city as the Indian residential areas were far out of town and the nature of my work meant that I usually finished late at night or in the early hours of the morning.

The two musicians, Wayne and Vic, were so excited that night that they hardly slept. They were particularly pleased because of the reception they'd received from a white audience, and because their own compilations had received ovations.

The next morning, when I left for the office, I told my guests to leave whenever they wished to.

That afternoon when I got home, Fakir was waiting in the corridor. I greeted him as usual and, without warning, he rushed up and punched me on the chin, which floored me! I got up all confused, while the neighbors tried to restrain him. Fakir was a short man with a huge ego and I could easily have taken him, but I kept wondering why, what had I done? I discovered when he screamed, "You had kaffirs staying here last night, and I want you out now!" That kind of derogatory language and naked racism from an Indian left me with no option but to pack up and leave immediately.

In all honesty, I was becoming disillusioned with the music business because I was operating at cross-purposes with my partners. My intent was to use music to unify South Africans but theirs was to use the unification mantra to make money.

I guess my idealism in this capitalist industry was not welcome and I had to consider leaving.

Having experienced the richness and diversity of South African music I wanted to put it all together. So I took Wayne and Vic to a farm house in Pietermaritzburg—a place with an abundance of greenery, where they teamed up with Graeme and Philip from my university band Betus. This was my final laboratory experiment. Philip played lead guitar in the style of Led Zeppelin, Graeme played drums with African influences, Wayne played a disco bass and Vic played disco rhythm.

I went back to my hometown, visiting them only on weekends. I left them on the farm for two months because I wanted them to live together and put together a truly authentic South African sound.

At the end of that time, we had a brilliant demo tape of a fusion of rock and disco, which Graeme and I took to virtually every record company in Johannesburg.

Finally, we landed in the office of Peter Gallo of Gallo Records, who thought it was an interesting crossover sound—a fusion of black and white music—but he was not keen to put any money into it.

He made it clear that he was there for business and had no time for "aesthetics," meaning that he would choose a traditional Zulu group over Dire Straits; although the latter produced great music, it was the former that brought in the money.

Exhausted and tired of having doors closed to us, Graeme and Philip left for London and formed a band called Timbuktu. Wayne & Vic tried to continue in Johannesburg but ended up parting ways.

Not long after this Michael Jackson (disco) and Eddie Van Halen (rock) got together to record their best-selling album *Thriller*—yet we had produced this sound in South Africa long before they did!

I surmised, philosophically, that we'd simply been ahead of our time.

After the music business, I took time off for self-reflection.

Always the idealist and obsessed with wanting to change the world, if not to only to make a difference, I obtained a scholarship to The Leadership Institute of South Africa—the brainchild of Professor Martin Nasser, Harvard visiting scholar and head of The University of South Africa's Business School, whose MBA was transformed into an MBL, with the emphasis on leadership.

We were a mixed bunch of South Africans, whom the Institute, through interviews and psychometric tests, determined possessed innate leadership qualities.

In short, Academia was now breaking apartheid boundaries, and I enjoyed the ride, especially meeting enlightened white academics with similar musical tastes—idealists, seeking change and a better place for All.

A year later, I married, we were expecting our first child and I needed a job.

When Radio 702 came on air, it was targeted around Johannesburg. It was licensed in the neighboring homeland of Bophuthatswana and transmitted from there. At night, the medium wave traveled further and bounced off the Drakensberg Mountains, which meant I could pick up the station clearly in my hometown of Weenen. I became an avid evening listener and admired the style of one of the DJs, Stan Katz, so I wrote him a letter and included my CV. In his reply he said there were no vacancies at the station, but he referred me to Hennie Pietersen of the SABC (South African Broadcasting Services), who was involved with Radio Lotus, a newly established station catering for the Indian community.

Radio Lotus had been launched only after Issie Kirsh had set up Radio Truro from neighboring Swaziland on a weak medium-wave band, targeting

South Africa's million Indians. The government-controlled SABC saw a radio station geared for Indians as an opportunity to promulgate its policy of separate development and started up one of its own, using a strong FM frequency. Radio Truro had been forced to close down, but after obtaining another medium wave frequency, Kirsh established Radio 702.

My interview was conducted by Isabel van der Linde, an old hand at radio; she was the "forces' favorite" in the days of Springbok Radio and went on to become the station manager for Radio Lotus. Isabel was impressed that I was a graduate and spoke good English. She was not very concerned that I spoke no Indian languages and knew little about Indian music.

On the musical score, I depended largely on my wife, Fozia, who had grown up on a diet of Indian movies and music because her uncles owned some cinemas in her hometown. She helped me with the pronunciation of song titles, which I often made a holy mess of. With time, I learned to announce the song title at the end, after having listened to it carefully. On the English side of Radio Lotus, I did the Saturday night Lotus line-up of the top-10 pop songs of the week, which became very popular with young listeners. I also read the news and did talk shows.

I had acceded to working for an Indian station, but this did not obliterate my rebellious nature. When the Dire Straits hit single "Sultans of Swing" was banned because the group donated the proceeds from their South African sales to the ANC, I took my own copy to the studio one night and played it. Boy, did I get into trouble for that! On another evening I played a song by The Police and said, "That was The Police, the most arresting band in the land."

Then, the one that proved to be the last straw: we had tons of paperwork to complete during and after each program, so I had to have a say (on air) about the bureaucracy, "One day in the future archaeologists will dig up this place and conclude that it was a paper manufacturing factory where workers were entertained with music."

From that moment, Isabel instructed me to script everything I was going to say and it had to be approved by an Afrikaner supervisor, Vossie van Buren. It seemed that where I was concerned, she was not willing to allow any leeway.

Being at Radio Lotus had been a valuable experience as it had put me in touch with my roots—the Indian community. I gained an appreciation for Indian music and also learned about ingrained forms of bigotry such as class and caste, as well as religious intolerance. These had been imported from India but were nurtured in Apartheid South Africa. That wasn't difficult because bigotry was a hallmark of the system; even institutionalized by law.

While on Radio Lotus, I did an audition for television as the SABC was on the verge of starting a program for Indians and needed continuity presenters, but from out of the blue the Department of Foreign Affairs approached me with a firm job offer.

To borrow from Bob Dylan, "The times they are a changing."

Some felt it was too slow, others felt too soon, whereas, I felt it was upon me to take the plunge to become the first career diplomat of color, and add my weight to smoothen the journey to real and effective change, leading to Freedom from apartheid.

So *diplomacy* called …

My first posting was to Los Angeles in 1988—where I caught up with music concerts, beginning with Bob Dylan at Hollywood Bowl, Rolling Stones at LA Colosseum, Bruce Springsteen and many others, guess the world's musicians came to LA and I was there.

Also through common musical tastes, I connected with a cross-section of West Coast Americans, and my stint at Radio Lotus enhanced my ability to communicate via radio and television to West Coast Americans, my vision of the change that was coming to South Africa.

I returned to South Africa in 1991, apartheid was buried on the scrapheap of history, the country was going through the birth pangs of Freedom and I was promoted to Spokesperson for the Department of Foreign Affairs—a most interesting time to be in the limelight of the world's focus.

The world then opened up—I went to Karachi in Pakistan to pioneer diplomatic relations in the land of my ancestors. There I facilitated a connection with Radio Pakistan for the manager of Radio Lotus, who was touring the country, to do a live broadcast. In those days, a phone connection from Karachi to Rome to Johannesburg, surmounted the boundaries, and the show went on, with me even doing a live presentation of music.

From Pakistan, I went to pioneer diplomatic relations with the Gulf, and landed in Abu Dhabi in the United Arab Emirates, and its where I first met Nelson Mandela. He had taken parts of the national anthems of the apartheid regime, and mixed it with parts of the anthem of the African National Congress. I had a very difficult time convincing the Abu Dhabi military band, the night before, to play parts of each score, but was rewarded for my efforts, when they performed to Mandela's joy, for doing it right.

Music was uniting a people divided, led by the legendary Mandela, healing the country with common and shared anthems.

Four years later, I went home to Freedom. Initially, I was doing media for international conferences, NAM and Commonwealth and then I landed up on the North Africa Desk in Foreign Affairs.

On one of my many travels to Cairo, I have to share a most interesting story.

Remember Wayne & Vic the colored guys who played to a white audience at Plumb Crazy in Johannesburg, then got me kicked out of my apartment, and they teamed up with two of my university band members to create the sound, that was rejected but made into a hit by Michael Jackson and Eddie Van Halen.

As I was going up to my room at the Hilton hotel in Cairo in Egypt I noticed a poster—Vic of Wayne and Vic had teamed up with an Italian and they were playing there.

That night, I walked into a packed nightclub, to witness, a South African colored, with an Italian belting out cover and original songs to the elite of Cairo society. When Vic caught my eye, he stopped in mid-song and said, "I can't believe it, the man who gave me a start in the music business is here. Raf, don't leave, we need to talk!" and then he continued.

During a break, we shared our stories, me being a diplomat and he pursing his musical dream in Cairo.

Arriving at the Hilton hotel in Tel Aviv I was met by Chris Borain, Primedia's finance manager, whose youthful looks belied his senior designation in the company. He had a friendly manner and, while chatting as he led me to where Issie was waiting in the restaurant, we established something in common—our passion for sport. I had seen photographs of Issie in newspapers, but when I met him, I was struck by his humility, warmth and sincerity. He was almost seventy, yet he looked good, seemed full of energy and was still actively involved in his business.

He began by thanking me for taking the time to meet him and then explained, "I was on a flight and came across a Time magazine article about Palestinian billionaire Munib Masri. I thought of meeting with him, to partner him in setting up a radio station in Amman, Jordan, to broadcast into the region, including Israel and Palestine." Issie knew it was virtually impossible to obtain a radio license in Israel itself and he therefore opted for the South African model with which he had so much success—the use of an adjoining country. This had led him to Amman, where he had seen another opportunity and ended up investing in a cinema complex in a joint venture with Jordanian businessmen, which they had called Ster Century. In his capacity as an investor in Jordan, Issie had then approached the South African ambassador in Amman for assistance in obtaining a radio license. Dr Vincent Zulu had apparently not even been aware that Primedia had invested in the cinema complex, but he also made it clear that he could not help. I surmised that, as a political appointee, Zulu had little experience of this aspect of being a diplomat. I was curious to know more about Primedia and learned that it owned the more than five hundred Ster-Kinekor cinemas in South Africa, as well as advertising billboards and other media outlets. I also found out that the company was listed on the Johannesburg Stock Exchange and that Issie—with his son William, who had taken over as CEO—had partnered with the National Union of Mineworkers. This was a truly viable business model that addressed the black economic empowerment requirements of the new South African government.

Getting back to his saga about trying to obtain a radio license, Issie said when the Jordan option had come to naught, he had approached Johann Marx, the South African ambassador in Tel Aviv, who had also made it clear he could not assist.

I interjected, "Issie, by being in Tel Aviv I am encroaching on Marx's turf. My responsibility as the South African representative in Palestine is the West Bank and the Gaza Strip. But, since Aziz Pahad referred you to me and I know he is familiar with my media background, I am here to meet you in that capacity." However, I stressed that my approach to diplomacy was not fixated on bureaucracy and rules, which I saw as guiding but not limiting. My successes to date, I added, were based on my adventurous spirit and on serving my country's interests by thinking and executing actions outside the box. Issie wanted to know about my media background. "It's strange how destiny has brought us together," I said. I told him how Stan Katz of Radio 702 had referred me to Hennie Pietersen at the SABC, which had led to my involvement in Radio Lotus in the 80's. I then asked what had inspired him to start an Indian radio station. Issie explained, "My brother Natie obtained a radio license from Swaziland and we learned that on a Saturday morning, for an hour, Radio Port Natal in Durban saw a meteoric rise in listeners because the government had provided an hour of radio time to the million plus Indians in the country. We saw a gap and thought a radio station dedicated to the Indians would be the way to go. The result was Radio Truro, the name of the first ship that ferried Indian laborers from India to South Africa." He reflected on the weak signal and immense problems they had faced but saw them as a learning curve that had propelled him to his next venture, Radio 702, which had quickly gained popularity. In the same leapfrog move as it had employed with Radio Lotus, the SABC had then set up Radio 5 on an FM frequency with national reach, as a countermeasure to 702. But Issie had not faltered against such a strong adversary. He had been brave enough to pioneer talk radio at a time when most thought it was fraught with danger. The timing was perfect as Radio 702 provided a space for South Africans, segregated by law, to talk about common issues. This had served to highlight our similarities and that we shared the same concerns.

It was fascinating to listen to this media icon talking about his passion which, after all these years, had still not waned. When I asked how I could help, he said, "I want to set up an English 702-type station from Ramallah, broadcasting into Israel, to get both sides to talk, in a neutral language, about common issues in the search for a peaceful solution to this senseless conflict." My immediate reaction was, "What an incredible idea!" It would add weight to all that I was doing as an ambassador, which was to support the peace process. This idea really promoted people-to-people diplomacy and I was sold.

Issie added, "I need your assistance in obtaining a radio license from the Palestinian side."

"I assure you I will do everything I can to get it for you and I am confident I'll succeed, because I have established contacts at the highest level."

Issie and I were finally linked by our common desire to use media to heal people in conflict. Somehow, in my bones, I had the feeling that destiny was charting a course and that a roller-coaster ride was on the cards. On my way back to Ramallah, I called my assistant, Maysoun and explained Issie's needs. She said, "I'll make calls and by the time you get here, will have something for you." And so, she did—Maysoun had spoken to the minister responsible for radio licenses, Yasser Abed Rabbo, with whom I had a good relationship. A meeting was scheduled for the next morning.

I immediately called Issie on his mobile phone to tell him the good news. I added, "I can attend the meeting on my own, but I suggest you and Chris join me. All you should do is get to Jerusalem. I live there and travel daily to Ramallah and you can come with me." It was 2003, the Second Intifada (Palestinian uprising against Israel) was at its peak and Issie was placing his life in my hands as we drove to Ramallah in the diplomatic car. Unlike other ambassadors, I always sat in the front seat, so my compatriots took the back seat. We drove with the South African flag (our safeguard) fluttering and I felt a sense of pride in that the three of us—representing the three monotheistic faiths of Jerusalem—were united in a single cause and could work together to achieve the outcome. It gave me hope for the Holy Land of conflict. As a diplomat, I had access to the road that Israeli settlers used, and which was barred to Palestinians from the West Bank—a form of apartheid, justified by Israel's security concerns. The route that Palestinians used could take forever with a checkpoint that, to put it mildly, created a torturous delay.

After passing through the military checkpoint leading into Ramallah my guests were confronted with the sight of a shelled City Inn hotel—a stark reminder that we were entering a war zone. Then we drove past President Arafat's Mukata'a (headquarters), which was smashed to rubble, save for a solitary building in which he was besieged and isolated. Issie and Chris were intrigued. After driving through the city center, which we did daily to pick up the morning newspapers, we arrived at the South African representative office—an impressive building in relation to those in the vicinity. My guests walked in with me to my office, where I introduced them to Maysoun, whom Issie thanked profusely for her assistance.

After coffee, we drove to Raboo's office. He was a member of the Palestinian Liberation Organization's executive committee and the minister of information and cabinet affairs—the right address to seek a radio license. After the introductions, Issie explained the role Radio 702 had played in building bridges in South Africa and how he wished to replicate the model in this part of the world. At the time, Raboo and Israeli politician Yossi Beilin were drafting a peace proposal, so he saw Issie's idea as a novel approach. Raboo assured us he would provide his support for the project. As we were leaving, Issie asked for Raboo's assurance in writing because he had to report back to the board of Primedia. Raboo said that by the time we got back to the embassy, it would have been faxed. For me, it was an assignment completed, but for Issie it was the first step to the realization of his dream and he couldn't stop thanking me. "I wish other ambassadors had the same attitude," he said.

"Issie, I am a professional career diplomat, I don't belong to any political party, I represent the government of the day, but I serve my country and its people. Your taxes pay my wages and I am only doing my duty."

To reciprocate for the lunch in Tel Aviv and to manifest a show of hospitality, as well as to celebrate our success, I invited Issie and Chris to lunch at the Bardoni Restaurant in Ramallah.

Seated in a leafy and picturesque establishment, I reminded them that the Israeli army could come into the city at any time, impose a curfew and begin military operations, but then assured them that as a diplomat with an official car nearby we could be escorted out safely—as my diplomatic immunity was provided by Israel, and the car bore Israeli diplomatic plates, since Palestine was not a state and the Oslo Accords which provided it interim authority, warranted this measure from the Israeli side. That was the worst-case scenario, which my guests were made aware of, but it mattered not.

During the lunch, Issie received a call from his son William in Johannesburg and when he told him that he was in Ramallah having lunch with the South African Ambassador, Issie related to us that William was simply dumbfounded. I learned that William had become an observant Jew, so I could imagine his concern for his dad but on the other hand, knowing Issie's adventurous and entrepreneurial spirit he may have understood.

Issie excitedly shared the good news with his son and assured him that he was in safe hands with me. I felt a sense of responsibility with the trust he had bestowed on me.

The next day Issie and Chris met Israeli minister Ehud Olmert and explained their vision for the project. Olmert, who went on to become prime minister, assured him of his support and added that since it was going to be in English, it would not pose a problem to Israeli radio stations broadcasting in Hebrew. Issie received Olmert's blessing and he was satisfied.

In the space of two to three days an English radio station serving Palestine and Israel was on the cards.

On Issie's return to South Africa, he instructed Dave Berndt a technical expert from Sentech the technical company Primedia dealt with, to fly in and get to Ramallah to complete the preparatory work.

A week later, Dave arrived, and we made all the necessary arrangements to have him picked up and taken by me to Ramallah, where my driver, Rageb, took him along for the day, as he obtained readings and looked at the topography to determine the best possible location for the transmitter and the size required, to cover Palestine/Israel. At the end of the day, his readings and analysis led him to suggest a certain part of the city. This he communicated to Issie with a detailed report on his return, but to me it all sounded Greek, that is, the technical jargon associated with radio transmission.

I realized then, Issie was serious about the project. I reported my excitement to my principals in South Africa. Here was a radio station that promoted dialogue and bridge-building. The station would supplement my diplomatic work. It would, as they say, "Support the peace process."

Little did I know at the time that a conspiracy to end my diplomatic career was brewing, but that is another story.

Back to the Radio 702 party in Sandton—

I met John Berks, the legendary South African radio talk show host and suggested to him, "Why don't you come out of retirement and do the morning show in Jerusalem?"

"Yes! Issie has spoken to me about it and I am thinking about it."

Thereafter we talked about the political situation and whether it was safe for John to come to Jerusalem and Ramallah. I assured him, "There may be a conflict, but somehow I feel safer there than in crime-ridden South Africa."

I then mingled with the other guests, and among them, I had the pleasure of meeting Stan Katz and reminded him as well as thanked him for his assistance in directing me to Hennie Pietersen of the SABC, as we spoke about the beginnings of my radio career. He could not remember, but nevertheless accepted the appreciation.

Maysoun, my Palestinian wife and I, also met up with Mark Klusener and his wife Peroshnee, both of whom had been to Israel and Palestine as journalists for ETV and "The Star" respectively, during my short-lived term as an ambassador there. After chatting with them, about the envisaged radio station, Mark indicated that he was very interested in joining us, should it materialize.

Back to the party, it was food, food and food and lots of speeches but the one that touched everyone was, when Issie who had just had a hip replacement operation had to be helped onto the stage to deliver his and the final speech of the event. He stood there, admired by all, and briefly explained his vision and how it was realized and then he thanked all who helped him along the way. This was Issie, a selfless and a totally generous human being, and he brought a tear or two not only to me but to many others as we listened to him.

He then received a standing ovation—here was a visionary who had, twenty-five years prior, taken on the apartheid government and literally blazed a trail in South African media with talk radio.

It was an inspiring moment and I felt enveloped in it, even convinced into believing that what Maysoun, Issie and I were attempting to do in Palestine and Israel was certainly doable.

That evening Maysoun and I, over dinner, talked about the radio project that she was consulting on and which had simply got bogged down.

Until then, Maysoun had used her network of contacts built during her eight years working with the South African mission in Ramallah. She had visited the relevant ministries to obtain the paperwork and requirements to fulfill, prior to the granting of the license, and on her return, she reported to Issie, who was generally satisfied with progress made.

In Sandton, Maysoun continued spending her time at the Primedia studios—sitting in on various shows, learning about the technical and production aspects of radio as well as interacting with the sales, marketing and management personnel. It was practical and hands-on learning and training for her and she was relishing every moment of it.

On the odd occasion, I met with either Chris Boraine or Yusuf Abramjee over coffee or lunch at the News Cafe, opposite Primedia, and we generally talked about progress and what was still needed to be done. My role was simply advisory, but I was happy that things were moving, albeit slowly.

On the many visits by Maysoun and Chris, I suggested that I accompany them for two reasons, firstly, I still held onto my diplomatic passport, through the ineptitude of ANC cadres in the protocol department, as well as the Israeli foreign ministry card, which facilitated easy entry and exit through the Israeli checkpoints and secondly my presence in meetings with the Palestinian government officials would, in a sense, intimidate and facilitate movement in the sluggish bureaucracy. As for costs to Primedia: all we did was to downgrade Maysoun's business class ticket to two economy ones, whilst Chris traveled in business class.

Maysoun and I were determined to make the radio station a reality and we were in no way inconvenienced with this minor discomfort. Maysoun's heart was still in Jerusalem. As for me, I felt duty-bound to complete what I had begun with Issie and what South African Foreign Affairs had prematurely curtailed.

I was philosophical. Traditional diplomacy was replaced by the role that instantaneous communication facilitated across the globe. Language had become the new battlefield, media was the artillery and words were the ammunition. Reality became the casualty. A radio station for Palestinians and Israelis could be the best prescription to heal the pain caused by the conflict.

On one visit, we learned that Samir Rantisi who eagerly wished to partner with Primedia and who did all that was asked of him locally in Ramallah was shot and killed outside his home by unknown gunmen and for reasons that were speculative in nature. Not only was a valuable local partner lost, it jolted us. We realized, suddenly, that this was a conflict and we were in a war-zone. The road was fraught with much difficulty.

Returning from that visit, both Chris and Maysoun reported developments to Issie who then recommended that on the next trip, Yusuf accompanied us to provide his input, as he possessed valuable knowledge and insights, as he was, station manager for Radio 702.

On that visit, a huge story broke out, the Israeli pull-out from the Gaza Strip, and Yusuf was in the right place at the right time. I watched him revel in reporting the world's biggest story from Jerusalem and Ramallah, with phone calls to Gaza. I even arranged an interview with a South African woman married to a Gazan who eventually went back to Cape Town.

As for the radio project, Yusuf advised on personnel requirements and studio equipment and even interviewed interested candidates. Mostly, it was on this trip that we all realized the importance of an English radio station, especially its relevance for news bulletins in a fast-developing story.

Interestingly, Yusuf learned from locals that my successor in Ramallah, Sisa Nkwane, an ANC cadre, had raped his Filipino maid and had left for South Africa, with the Israelis preventing his return. South African Foreign Affairs had tried to sweep this story under the carpet and had quietly transferred Sisa to Angola. Yusuf broke the story in South Africa on Radio 702 and created much embarrassment for the department. Sisa eventually died of AIDS somewhere in Africa.

Meanwhile, Primedia was having much difficulty in investing in the project, which at that stage, moved along on a letter of support from minister Abed Raboo. Issie understood from me that it was the way things were done in Palestine. To address everyone's concerns, we then arranged a meeting with President Arafat and used the occasion to explain to him the nature of the radio project and the credentials of Primedia. He responded, "South Africa, *Ahlan wa Sahlan!*" meaning Welcome!

Arafat personally blessed this project and that was it! Armed with photographs capturing the occasion, Chris returned to Primedia to confront the skeptics, especially the CEO, Terry Shapiro who was dead against the project.

After this, everything went quiet for a while.

It was on a follow-up trip via Dubai, I arranged to meet with my good friend Anwar Sher, who was the CEO of the ruling family's bank during my pioneering diplomatic stint in the UAE. Anwar had moved on to head the huge Dubailand project. In his office, he bragged about the mega construction projects his company was involved in and how I missed out on his offer to join him after the completion of my diplomatic tour of duty and to drive home his point, he picked up the phone and spoke, "Come to my office, I have a surprise for you."

In came the former British ambassador, Tony Harris, who had taken the job offered to me as their PRO, "Hello Rafique, how are you?"

I was surprised to see him there.

We then learned from our conversation with Tony Harris, who during my term in Abu Dhabi, always asked Anwar, "Why does the royal family treat Rafique so differently?" and Anwar would generally respond, "He is a super diplomat." Tony was not aware that besides my diplomatic skills, I had an uncle (Sheik Ahmed Deedat) who was respected as an Islamic scholar by the ruling family.

When I informed Tony that my successor, Saloojee, was promoted and now South Africa's ambassador to Iran, and briefed him on the circumstances that led to my recall from Ramallah for capacity building he expressed total disbelief, a sentiment shared by Anwar, who was close to the ruling family and who also had the highest respect for my diplomatic skills, manifest in tangible successes during my tour of duty in the UAE.

Tony then related stories about Saloojee. "He was always falling asleep at diplomatic meetings and even snoring aloud," Tony said, "and his night-time sexual adventures were legendary among the diplomatic corps." Tony then added, "All the magnificent work you did Rafique, this guy blew it!" I smiled and shrugged my shoulders, "Sad but true."

Meanwhile, living in Sandton, with its materialistic indulgence and hedonistic lifestyle was beginning to wear Maysoun and me down and it soon began to create a sense of restlessness.

We sought something meaningful, something that made a difference to people's lives. Because both of us believed—Isn't love supposed to be the highest form of rebellion, a fight for something totally new? Its purity ought not to be based on virginity, but on beauty, trust, determination and courage and for imagination, the ability to dream, the desire to fight for a much better world!

The morning after the 702 party, we went to see Issie at his home in Sandhurst. We were welcomed by his wife Moshe, who seated us in the living room. Soon, we were joined by Issie, who seemed to be in much pain as he was helped along by a nurse. Coffee was served, and we began chatting about the radio project, as we brought him up to speed on developments which he may have missed out on, having been in hospital for a while.

Maysoun and Issie were then engaged in discussion and eventually I interjected, "Issie if you want this radio station to get off the ground, give us three months and I promise you, you will have it up and running."

This is when Issie's face lit up and he said, "Okay I give you guys three months, go and set it up, I am behind you."

It was a done deal, Maysoun and I would return to the Holy Land with a challenge on our hands.

We were later joined by Dr Ali Bacher, Issie's brother-in-law, who dropped in to see him. I had met Ali before in Karachi, when he headed South African cricket and I was the consul general there, and as a former cricketer myself, I had the greatest admiration for Ali, especially for his successes on the field as well as off the field for the leadership role he played in the transformation of South African cricket. He had been informed by Issie about the radio project. Ali thought it to be an amazing idea.

Seated with two Jewish icons from media and sport, with a Palestinian wife and being Muslim, mattered not. We were all beyond the issues of race and religion that had perpetuated an intractable conflict in the Holy Land, we kept our eye on the ball and focused on using radio to build bridges of understanding—as music has no boundaries.

Back at our humble apartment, we immediately began making necessary arrangements to relocate to the Holy Land, on a new mission, something that gave me reason to be alive again, it even brought back meaning to my life—so different from what I was beginning to detest in Sandton, a self-indulgent and hedonistic existence with black entrepreneurs flaunting their connections to the ANC and white business persons inflating their egos. This was not the South Africa we all struggled for and I really felt uncomfortable living in the land of my birth.

Unlike my diplomatic postings of the past, where the state paid for the shipment of personal goods, in this instance we had to literally give away almost all our belongings, and left South Africa with only our clothes and a few essentials like books. Most of our belongings were taken, with gratitude, by Lydia, our helper, who was a Zimbabwean economic refugee and with whom Maysoun had built a meaningful friendship.

Before departing, we met with deputy minister Aziz Pahad, at his office in the Union Buildings in Pretoria. Walking up the stairs and inside, I showed Maysoun where I had begun my diplomatic career and the offices I had occupied along the way, in this majestic building—the seat of power in South Africa.

As we walked through the hallowed corridors I reminisced on eventful and historic times.

We then entered the office of the deputy minister. Seated, we informed him about the radio project and especially the vision, which he understood and fully endorsed. He even assured us of his personal support.

Then over tea he inquired, "How is your case against foreign affairs going?"

Affidavits were being transmitted between both parties, a forerunner to an eventual high court hearing.

After saying our respective goodbyes, he surprised us: "I didn't say it, but fuck the department!" Aziz was saying he was aware but powerless to rectify the gross injustice that had been meted out to me by a senior and inept official who had abused his powers in a department that I had faithfully served for seventeen years.

But, with fissures developing daily in the body-politic of South Africa and the country slowly sinking into an abyss, I felt it in my bones that it was time to head back to the Holy Land of conflict, to embark on another adventure.

Yes! The Middle East was beckoning, with something far bigger and more challenging than diplomacy. It was going to be a marriage of diplomacy and media, the two loves of my life. I was up for it!

2 Building A Radio Station

A labor of love in a land of conflict

W<small>E ARRIVED IN</small> T<small>EL</small> A<small>VIV ON THE EVENING</small> of 30th September 2005—we had three months in which to put together a radio station, possessing no technical expertise whatsoever, but the firm assurance from Issie that he was behind us 100% and available 24/7—at least that was comforting.

Dawood, a taxi-driver from Jerusalem, who bore a striking resemblance to the Hollywood actor, Richard Gere, picked us up from Ben Gurion airport and drove us to Ramallah, through the congested Kalandia checkpoint. He had been with us all through the evolution of the radio project, listening to our discussions as he drove us to and from meetings—"I am so excited that it is all coming together. I lived and worked in New York and I can't wait to listen to English music in my taxi."

Looking out the window and reflecting on the journey as the vistas offered by the surrounding hills of Jerusalem flashed by, somehow made me believe that destiny had played a hand, more so that this was the Holy Land after all.

Arriving in Ramallah, we moved directly into our furnished apartment in the Al Tireh neighborhood, a lush green part of the city, nestled in rolling hills and picturesque valleys, dotted with olive groves. The apartment was tastefully furnished by the landlady for a young banker who spent some weekends there, until he was tragically killed in a terrorist bombing at a hotel in Amman in Jordan. I saw some photographs of him in the room that housed his office and wondered, what a waste of a promising life!

Welcomed by a hot shower, we soon settled into bed in one another's arms, and wondered what lay ahead, as a new beginning beckoned with much hope in a land divided by a bloody conflict. And after planting the seed that would grow to be our beloved child, we then talked about the other child that we had to create and build. We were there to play a role in building bridges of understanding through music and talk and hopefully to lend a hand in the search for a peaceful solution to an intractable conflict.

Thereafter, our thoughts went back to the time I had invited Maysoun to dinner at my residence in Jerusalem in appreciation for coming to my aid with food during an earlier snow storm. We recalled how we spent the better part of the evening going through my music collection and finding common artists and songs, relating moments of our lives to those times. Little did we know where it was all leading to.

Exhausted we soon fell asleep.

In the morning, we began in earnest—just the two of us—to secure premises, buy and transport a transmitter and antenna systems from Israel to Ramallah, build the tower, install all the technical components, fit a basic studio, secure a frequency and then begin a test transmission to obtain the license. We had three months to achieve all of this and we began to work 24/7 to meet the deadline—a challenging task in a most difficult environment—subject to Israeli incursions, closures and during an ongoing bloody conflict.

Nevertheless, the challenge and task of setting up a radio station had begun in earnest. Firstly, there was the bureaucratic track—although in principle we had obtained the green light from the president himself, we still had to complete all the necessary paperwork and fulfill the stipulated requirements set-out by the government ministries concerned: information, telecommunications and security.

In Palestine, many radio stations operated illegally. We were determined to be totally legal and transparent and to pay all fees and dues. We sought to be legit, period!

The second challenge was to set-up the basic infrastructure of the radio station: and then begin test transmission, before the license proper was issued. This was necessary, as one could easily obtain a license (paper) and then flog it for a profit.

The question that our detractors in Primedia in Sandton always posed—what guarantee was there that once the transmission was operational, the license would be granted? There was absolutely none. It was just word of mouth. Now tell that to the executives and shareholders of Primedia in Johannesburg, who were overtly skeptical of the project from its inception but reluctantly went along because of Issie and wished it never materialized.

Maysoun and I began by visiting the three ministries, all of whom she had cultivated excellent relationships with, whilst she was with the South African representative office in Ramallah, and having me along as the former South African ambassador, added weight to the cause, if not intimidated the junior officials in the bureaucracies.

I observed how Maysoun made men in all these male-dominated ministries uneasy, as they were not accustomed to having a woman, albeit a westernized one married to a South African, putting together an international media project. When some of them even tried to thwart her efforts, I made my presence more than visible.

After days of tirelessly running around from office to office and to many buildings around town, we finally obtained all the relevant paperwork and completed all the prerequisites but somehow, we obtained a sense that some officials smelled a conspiracy which then manifested itself into a sense of reluctance and stalling. We nevertheless knew from the onset that this was one of the many challenges we had to surmount.

Our dining room table at home served as the office, with a laptop and piles of paper on it, and every evening Maysoun briefed Issie on the day's happenings and progress via a lengthy telephonic conversation.

Then there was the issue of finding a suitable location, to place the transmitter there, erect the tower for the antennae systems and then build the actual studios and offices—indeed a mammoth task—as both of us lacked technical knowledge pertaining to radio, which was exacerbated by the conflict, regular closures of the West Bank by the Israeli army and lack of access to human expertise and material needs.

Nevertheless, we soldiered on; and not long after, we found a most suitable building—the Al Jamil Center—located near the mukata or presidency and from the rooftop, one could see Tel Aviv, a perfect location for the transmitter. Also, there was a small building on the roof itself, to house the transmitter.

Maysoun then negotiated the lease for the 4th floor, to use for the studios and offices. Liaising with Issie on the phone and via email, we arranged it all in a relatively short space of time.

So, a place, we had!

The transmitter was another issue—Palestinians cannot import transmitters, barred by Israel. But there was a way around this hurdle. Sergey, a Russian Jew had an operation in Haifa, where he used discarded Israeli army equipment to assemble transmission equipment which he then sold to radio stations both in Israel and Palestine. He operated through his agent, Jihad in Ramallah, and with whom he had studied in the former Soviet Union. And they had a transportation guy, Mansoor, who smuggled in these transmitters, late at night. Obviously, Sergey worked with the Israeli army and there was no doubt that the latter were aware of his modus operandi.

This was the only option available to us, and even to Israeli radio stations like Radio Haifa and Tel Aviv, where Issie was a shareholder. We ordered a 3-kilowatt transmitter, as per the instructions of Sentech, the South African company, as well as the antennae systems they had recommended.

In the meantime, we had to build the tower on the roof of the building to house the antennae systems. Jihad brought along two local guys to do the job, but Maysoun and I kept at them all the time, only to learn that they were contend on taking ages to complete the job and we finally relieved them of the task. We then located another blacksmith, Abu Samir, whom we visited at his premises to learn that he was involved in building the towers for a local cellular company and his workmanship was excellent. I noted with a wry smile, that his wife called the shots, even negotiating the whole deal.

Watching my wife and his, I surmised with a wry smile—the sisters were doing it for themselves borrowing from the Eurhythmics and the Annie Lennox hit song.

Maysoun then fell pregnant which led us to make regular visits to Israeli gynecologists in Jerusalem, who found it strange—a South African of Indian ancestry married to a Palestinian and together they were setting up a radio station with a South African Jew, two babies conceived and growing into being simultaneously.

Not long thereafter, the transmitter arrived, and the tower was ready for installing the antennae systems. Abu Samir did the necessary, although it took two full days to complete. Then it was Jihad's turn to connect the transmitter to the antennae systems and right there and then . . . he blew it!

That was when we realized that Jihad was masquerading as a radio technician when he was clueless. Maysoun and I had no option but to terminate his services.

We then jumped into our hired car and drove north to Haifa to see Sergey, to meet with him at the offices of Radio Haifa, to make him understand that we were not just another Palestinian mickey mouse radio station.

Danny at Radio Haifa, also a partner with Issie on Radio Tel Aviv, arranged the meeting. He explained to Sergey, the station was Issie Kirsch's and Sergey had to pay special attention.

During the discussion, we learned much about radio transmission and about the issue of pirates both in Israel and Palestine, clogging up the frequencies, exacerbated by the interference created by regional radio stations from Lebanon in the north and Jordan in the south. A frequency war was raging in the region!

Sergey assured us that he would repair the damaged transmitter as soon as possible.

Most importantly, we learned that Jihad had forgotten to install three-phase electrical wiring which we immediately went about rectifying on our return to Ramallah.

Eventually, we received the repaired transmitter, and late one night, with the assistance of a local electrician and an extended cell-phone conversation with instructions from Sergey in Haifa, we managed to hook it up and switch it on. Then with the use of a computer with music loaded on it, we began with the test transmission on 93.6 FM, the frequency we chose after driving around the West Bank and Israel and opting for one of the many recommended by Sergey. It was relatively free of interference.

The first song that went on air was "Electric Avenue" by Eddie Grant, a very appropriate one to test the electrical transmission, and believe me it was not by choice—but a good omen nonetheless.

We then obtained music from Radio Highveld in Johannesburg via DHL and inserted it into the computer system, music interspersed with regular announcements—"You are listening to a test broadcast on 93.6 FM"—as we still had to obtain the license proper and then find a suitable name for the station.

In less than three months, we succeeded in broadcasting the test transmission—playing only music, with our signal reaching Tel Aviv, Amman in Jordan, and Gaza City in the south. All this because Maysoun and I worked together, surmounting numerous hurdles in our quest to realize Issie's dream of having an *ala Radio 702* in the Holy Land of conflict.

And I was not even paid a single penny for my part, as it mattered not to me, because my belief was that the idea was far bigger than any monetary reward whatsoever.

Issie and his son, William, then arrived on a weekend in Jerusalem. I met them at the King David Hotel and then drove them, still with my diplomatic card, which played a significant role in facilitating ease of movement, into Ramallah, to view our humble beginnings. I shall never forget, the excitement expressed by William when he observed the beginnings of our radio station and asked his father "Is this how you started Radio 702?"

Issie just nodded with delight that his dream was being realized.

William then used a Kodak disposable camera, which he had purchased at his hotel, to take photographs of the place and of all of us.

As we drove back to Jerusalem, we listened to the station on the car radio, to a signal that was subject to lots of interference and still needed fine-tuning, but we were on our way.

After my guests disembarked and we parted ways, I drove back to Ramallah reflecting on a most interesting morning but with a firm instruction from Issie, "Fix the signal!"

So, to meet the challenge posed by the inadequate signal or let's say— signal subject to interference by pirate radio stations, especially a Palestinian one, situated in Hebron—higher than Ramallah and with a better reach to Jerusalem, where our signal was at its weakest, we arranged to meet with

Issie, Maysoun and Keith inspecting the building of the radio tower

the management of Radio Tel Aviv and Radio Haifa to learn about practical options in seeking a solution from their experiences.

Maysoun and I then drove to Radio Tel Aviv studios, housed in a building in the newly renovated and hip port area. Such a lovely view of the Mediterranean ocean from the studios and I thought indeed a wonderful place with lots of creative energy flows, with a sea breeze wafting through the open office windows. We learned from the station manager and technical engineer that their signal was limited to the Tel Aviv area and could not go beyond. Anyway, they too were subject to regular interference from a radio station in the Gaza Strip and they were also helpless. So, our problem was not unique.

Next stop was Radio Haifa, housed in the middle of a huge shopping mall, which I found different from Radio Tel Aviv and if not interesting. The Two Dannys as Maysoun and I called them, and who owned the station, were very commercially oriented and they had made a tremendous success of their project. They too had problems with their signal, and faced the challenge of the mountainous terrain and interference from Lebanese radio stations. In the end, they opted to increase their transmitter capacity and suggested we do the same.

We were then joined by Sergey, and after listening to our problem, he indicated that he was very much aware of it. I got the feeling that he had a pretty good handle on the radio environment. His solution in the frequency war as he referred to it, was for us to purchase a larger transmitter and drown out the interference which Radio Haifa had successfully done. Sergey's suggestion was that we increase the transmitter's power from the present 3KW to 10KW, which would then give us strength as well as reach. Also, we would have to add more antennas to the existing ones on the tower. Then the three KW transmitter could be kept as a back-up whenever needed. We were sold on his suggestion but we considered it costly. However, when we called Issie and explained it all to him, he agreed to the purchase, and the order was immediately placed with Sergey.

Driving back to Ramallah, Maysoun and I spoke about how much we were learning about the technical aspects of radio transmission and believed that the suggested solution would enable us to solve the signal problem and then we could launch the station.

We had come a long way, in such a brief period.

Then it was time for Maysoun to take a break and stay at home, as she was in the final stages of her pregnancy. On doctor's orders, I took over from that point onwards—still with no financial remuneration, but driven by passion and a commitment to make the radio station a reality.

Dwelling on some of the other technical difficulties we faced and how we tried to surmount them—to begin with, there was a regular disruption of electricity from Jerusalem to Ramallah and it meant that we had to monitor the radio 24/7 and we had to very often and at strange times of the day and night, to physically go to the building, walk-up to the transmitter room, to reset the transmitter and computer and then to place the music back on track. To solve this, we fitted a UPS and then Issie recommended we order a diesel-powered electrical generator, which we did, from Turkey via a local agent.

Interference by other stations, especially an illegal one based in Hebron, created havoc with the signal, especially in Jerusalem, as Hebron is stationed higher than Ramallah. With a small portable radio in our company 24/7, we monitored the quality of the test signal, as we traveled around the West Bank and Israel, only to learn that we were still not there and certainly not ready to launch.

On the bureaucratic level—we had set-up the radio station, begun with the test transmission and then it was time for the ministry of telecommunications to issue us a license, as the other ministries had already given their approval, but not after many, many meetings and much discussions and loads of convincing. They had ascertained that Issie was a Jew and with that conspiracy theories gained currency especially that the radio station sought to sanitize or normalize the Israeli occupation of their land. My presence, as the former South African ambassador at these meetings generally took the wind of the sails of these unfounded theories.

Then on the morning on which we went to the ministry of telecommunications to pick-up the license, I was busy cooking lunch, and since Maysoun was pregnant, with doctors advising us not to let her drive, I took to the wheel, thinking that all it would take for us to get there and be back, would be about fifteen minutes, but it was not to be. A junior official at the ministry showed Maysoun a letter written by his senior and addressed to the minister, wherein the former recommended the license not to be issued.

This was serious!

I then put on my diplomatic hat and called Samir Hulileh, a friend who was then secretary to the Palestinian cabinet and asked him to arrange a meeting, as a matter of urgency, with the minister of telecommunications, which he immediately did.

Maysoun and I then walked into the office of Dr Sabri Saidam, a youthful looking minister, educated in the UK and who spoke fondly of joining anti-apartheid protests outside the South African embassy in Trafalgar square in London. I explained our radio project in detail to him, especially what our intentions were. He did not need much convincing, my bona fides as the former South African ambassador sufficed. Additionally, his best friend turned out to be Maysoun's cousin.

Right there and then, he approved the granting of the license, and we had won the first round of many battles to come. The license was issued in December 2005.

Returning home after many hours, we learned that we could have been homeless, as we just made it back in the nick of time and prevented what could have been a disastrous fire set off by the kitchen gas stove. After much mopping and cleaning up, we were finally relieved. The physical as well as metaphorical fires were taken care of and we could then relax. We eventually sat on the floor, exhausted and reflected on the amazing struggle to set-up the radio station and to then obtain the license, but in the end, it was all worth it.

Maysoun excitedly shared the good news with Issie in an extended telephone conversation—before the deadline of three months, we had set-up a radio station and had obtained a license.

Up to this stage, I had lent a helping hand, without any monetary reward whatsoever for my labor, political connections, PR and the use of my diplomatic passport and Israeli ID card to facilitate entry and exit of South Africans, including Issie, to and from Ramallah. During this call, Issie acknowledged my role and immediately arranged for Keith Gimrey, who was now his "point man" to negotiate a "consultancy contract" with me, for a token fee.

Keith Gimrey had replaced Chris Borain, as the latter left South Africa for Australia, after him and his wife and young daughters became victims of the crime that had ravaged the country, even though they lived in a heavily guarded security housing complex in Johannesburg.

Keith, who lived in Cape Town, was taken out of retirement by Issie and brought on board. He was a tall, slim man with gray hair and with English gentlemanly manners. He had begun his radio career with capital radio in the UK and joined Issie as his finance man, during the phenomenal growth of Primedia, eventually making way for a new generation, but he continued playing a role as a mentor. He was an experienced and no-nonsense bottom-line guy. In short—Keith knew his way around the radio business.

I watched him in action, as he facilitated, on his first trip to Jerusalem/Ramallah/Tel Aviv, the formation of the company, which Chris faffed around with for ages, and I was impressed.

Now the real work had to begin, work on building the studio, before we could rock 'n' roll!

Issie had this vision of replicating whatever that was done in Ramallah in Jerusalem, with Palestinians in one city and Israelis in the other, working together, and he made an earnest effort in this regard. He attempted to recruit the former director general from the Israeli second authority, a body responsible for radio in Israel, as Maysoun's equivalent—meaning two station managers on either side of the divide.

However, she was not convinced of the idea, and I recall Issie even saying to her, "I am a Zionist, but I believe this is the only way we can ensure our survival. How can we prosper when our neighbors do not?"

I appreciated Issie's honesty but I soon learned that Israelis, in the main, were not in tune with his vision. Issie eventually had to drop his idea of replication.

What impressed me most about Issie was that he was driven by a vision but maintained an open mind on the road to take to get there. He continuously changed strategy, tack and routes, but he was determined to reach his goal, of launching the radio station, no matter what. I appreciated this flexibility, after having myself worked in a stifling bureaucracy for the better part of my life. And it was fuel for me and did I tank it up,

While Issie was in the process of finding the right business partners, Palestinians and Israelis, to team up with, I had the pleasure of meeting with Ami, an Israeli involved in television, one evening at The American Colony hotel, in Jerusalem. Ami explained to me his reason for seeking peace—"I have a genius of a daughter. When she was a little girl, she would disappear in the mall and we would always find her in the bookshops, sitting on the floor reading. She completed high school and went into the army. You know with her genius what she does? She is in the demolition unit, blowing up homes of Palestinians whom we consider terrorists and making families homeless and guess what she does in the holidays; she works with orphans in South America. Raf, we live in a fucked-up place, when my girl thinks it's all right with what she is doing!"

This was the first time I had heard an Israeli questioning the absurdity of the Occupation. I really appreciated Ami's honesty and for him to share his concerns with me. This interaction enhanced my belief in the absolute necessity of the radio station to play the envisaged role.

Keith successfully put together the company. Issie wished to have a trilateral company—South Africans, Israelis and Palestinians. The South African component was made up of himself as the chairman, Primedia, Keith whom Issie gave shares to and Issie's brother Natie. The Israeli side comprised of Broadcast Holdings, the company involved with Radio Tel Aviv and this brought on board Tami Gothlieb, the chairperson of Radio Tel Aviv and Danny Anon, one of the directors of Radio Haifa, and then there was Jacob Perry, former head of the Israeli Shin Bet (Secret Police) and at the time, chairman of Mizrahi bank and Cellcom amongst the many companies on whose boards he sat. The lawyer who put this whole thing together was Asher (Cookie) Rabinowitz, an ex-South African, who took care of all Issie's business interests in Israel.

On the Palestinian side, Maysoun brought on board the two Nasiruddin brothers, Talal and Jalal, leading businessmen who I learned were very good friends with Jacob and that alone spoke volumes about money and profit having no borders.

Cookie registered the company—Middle East Radio as well as the offshore holding company based in Cyprus, a clever way to move envisaged profits out, I surmised!

Driving Maysoun and myself, was the envisaged social and political ramifications of radio programming and not the profits that may accrue from it for the business partners.

Nevertheless, after expanding much in the way of the proverbial, blood, sweat and tears, we now had a transmitter playing music, a license for a radio station and a trilateral company formed, with shareholders putting in monies to build the studios and offices.

We were then tasked to set-up studios in Ramallah and Jerusalem with a microwave link between the two cities. This meant that we would broadcast from Ramallah and with the linkage to Jerusalem we would be able to produce programming from there. The intent was to have both Palestinians and Israelis in respective studios to interact with the other, through the medium of radio, at a time when checkpoints and walls were increasingly separating them.

Maysoun and I continued to drive around and monitor both the reach and quality of the signals. We found it wanting, as we traveled further away from the source of transmission. The issue was this: Israel / Palestine is a small piece of land, with the FM frequency occupied by both sides, and by a sizable number of pirates. As everyone believed, possession is nine tenths of the law. And in this quagmire, regional radio stations compounded matters with additional interference in this small territory.

In short, the FM frequency bandwidth was in a holy mess!

Although Sergey had repaired the transmitter, it was forever crashing, and I would be at the premises, at odd times of the day and night, to restart it. Eventually the building janitor, Mohanat, who spoke no English and who always accompanied me to the roof of the building, figured out what needed to be done and he then took the initiative to relieve me of a huge burden. He was provided with a small transistor radio and thereafter took care when the transmission went down, save for days when his efforts failed. Then we had to resort to calling Sergey on the phone and with the assistance of a local electrician to try and figure out and fix whatever the problem was.

Sergey, as an Israeli, could not come to Ramallah, and we had no technical expertise in the city, which hampered us immensely, but it was not going to stop us.

To build the studios in Ramallah, we employed a local company that apparently had done similar work in the city, but when we were visited one weekend by Jaco, a young South African technical expert from Primedia in Sandton, we learned of major shortcomings and deficiencies. Apparently, locals had no clue about professional studio construction, especially about insulation and the general workmanship was shoddy. As South Africans, our standards were first world whilst in Palestine, the whole notion of victimhood relating to Occupation led to work that was wanting in more ways than one.

Maysoun and I continuously admonished the contractor and his workers, as we sought excellence.

After Jaco pointed out all the deficiencies that we had to attend to, and which we noted, we then drove him to Bethlehem—as a Christian he wished to visit the holy city. On the way, we monitored the signal and Jaco provided useful advice on what was causing the interference and how we ought to address it, which we attempted to do on his departure.

Issie visited the next time with John Berks (Berkowitz) whom he had persuaded to come out of retirement. John, with the aid of his agent had cleverly negotiated a very lucrative deal for himself: with accommodation, mobile phone costs and even laundry thrown into the deal, all the while making Issie believe he was reluctantly doing so.

On the other hand, Issie was getting serious about launching the station, but his vision called for replication in Jerusalem of what we had done in Ramallah. Basically, he wanted a studio in Jerusalem, providing the rationale that guests who couldn't go to Ramallah be interviewed there. The spin-off would be that both sides could talk on the phone to the guests from the other side. Wonderful way to bridge the divide!

John Berks then professed a kind of holiness and behaved like a diva. He wore the *kippah* when it suited him, but ate shrimps at our home when no Jew was looking. He insisted on having a studio close to the old city of Jerusalem. Issie, then settled for premises with David of R&R, a television company, but later dropped it when we learned that John's view would be obstructed by a building under construction. (This, after I went through a great deal of preparatory work with the architect, a pleasant lady by the name of Noah.) More valuable time was thus wasted by John's childish tantrums.

Eventually we settled for premises in the Technology Park Building in Malcha, opposite the Jerusalem Mall. Maysoun and I were invited to dinner by a young couple, Nicholas, an English Jew and Lipika a Bengali. (Whom I had met on a flight from Tel Aviv to Johannesburg.) At the dinner, we met journalists who were about to begin work at the Al Jazeera-English studios. They then introduced us to Arik and his partner, their service providers: Contact Solutions.

On meeting Arik, I was impressed with his positivity and passion. He immediately came along with his team to Ramallah—the Israelis all had media cards, which gave them access to Ramallah—to evaluate our technical issues. After seeing it first-hand, Arik assured us that he would sort all our problems so that we could focus our energies on programming and other issues related to the radio business.

Arik visited us with his trusted team of Israelis and Palestinians and it was such a pleasure to watch them work together, communicating only in Hebrew, which the Palestinians spoke fluently. Schmulik climbed up the tower and screamed to Faris below in Hebrew, and with it all happening right next door to the presidential compound, which was always teaming with security and intelligence personnel, was indeed surreal. Arik then assured us that his experience with Al Jazeera gave him the edge and he would use the existing microwave link to connect us with Jerusalem and their own operation there.

This was indeed the solution we sought, if not the answer to our prayers. Visiting their premises, we learned that their operation was highly professional. It served not only Al Jazeera television but other international media, as well.

From a diplomat / ambassador to a DJ

Soon, I had a lease signed on behalf of Issie and the premise in Malcha began to be fitted-up for our needs by a very able and dedicated team of interior designers. The energy that Arik's company manifested was indeed uplifting to us. The largest benefit: Our woes with the technical problems were now in the hands of experts.

Then in 2006, we suffered many hiccups—Maysoun took time off to deliver Adam, the second Lebanon war broke out, our new transmitter was stuck in Haifa for about three months—a city under constant rocket attack, and a host of unforeseen events stalled progress, but it gave us time to complete the building of the offices and studios both in Ramallah and Jerusalem.

In Maysoun's absence I was playing a greater role and my visibility had increased substantially—thus I was constantly questioned by Palestinians from various strata of society whom I had met during my short-lived diplomatic stint. Was this an exercise in normalization of the Occupation or not? I took great pains to explain, but I am afraid that I was not always successful.

Pioneers are always treated with suspicion as they chart new or disruptive courses or sometimes change what was deemed the rule. Often they pay a price for doing so. History has numerous examples, my own as South Africa's first diplomat of color and the trail I had blazed in the USA, Asia, the Middle East, and at home in Israel / Palestine was one that was beset with much criticism at the time.

Nonetheless, our efforts in building a radio station in Palestine and Israel had the blessing of Mandela on the South African side, Arafat on the Palestinian side, and Olmert in Israel. We were totally convinced that media that built bridges was an important route in the search for peace. Nothing was going to stop us.

Adam was born on 24 June 2006, at the Hadassah hospital in Jerusalem, delivered by a lovely American-Jewish midwife, as it was the Shabbat (Saturday afternoon) and doctors were mostly away. The next day, I had a string of rabbis, all marketing their respective skills and all wanting to circumcise Adam, some even proving that they knew the Quranic prayers that went along with it. I found this rather amusing, but informed all that we would do it later and with a pediatric surgeon. I was surprised: I experienced a hospital that catered to both Palestinians and Israelis with doctors from both sides attending to the other. "Why couldn't this permeate segments of society? I thought. "Perhaps our radio station will be a means to promote this very end."

Getting back to developments related to the radio station: Issie recruited and we were soon joined by two South African journalists, Andrew Bolton and Mark Klusener. They helped us set-up the news room, and they also recruited and trained both Palestinian and Israeli staff in all aspects of radio news reporting. Andrew, who had obtained radio experience with capital radio in the homeland of Transkei and then Radio 702, was a consummate professional. He had gone through a divorce and was starting over. Mark who had television experience under his belt, returned to the region with his sweetheart, Peroshnee, to set-up home in Ramallah.

They recruited Abdullah Erekat, Shireen Yassin, and Asherah Ramadan in Palestine and Tyson Herbeger in Israel. Then, they followed-up with intensive training led by Andrew.

We found Andrew, Mark, and Peroshnee a furnished apartment on the rooftop of the building where we lived. It was nice to have fellow South Africans with us in Ramallah.

Primedia was still not sold on the project. They only paid lip-service. So Issie engaged Peter Butler, an Australian radio consultant, who in turn recruited two Australians: Peter Tarnawski (music manager) and Barry Hill (DJ). Both were seasoned radio professionals. Peter had worked on radio in Sydney and, on arrival, he immediately got down to setting up the clocks and programming. Barry, a most likable guy from Newcastle moved into an apartment in our building.

The team was almost complete and we were getting ready to rock 'n' roll.

3 Launch of 93.6 Ram FM

A pioneering English radio station in Palestine/Israel

A ND THEN JOHN BERKS (BERKOWITZ) arrived to host the all-important breakfast show and to finally launch the station.

The Ramallah studios were ready and the personnel were all in place, including all the locally recruited administrative and support staff. Arik and his team had installed the new transmitter which was finally delivered to us at the end of the second Lebanon war. As a result, our signal had improved remarkably, and we were ready to rock 'n' roll!

Issie, true to form, was going to launch the station in style, but before doing so, we had to first find a suitable name.

At a shareholder's meeting which Issie chaired and at which I volunteered to take minutes, the name "RAM FM" was bandied around and eventually accepted by all. It has a good sound: 93.6 RAM FM.

Then, Issie flew-in Melanie Millen-Moore from Johannesburg. She came to the party with years of knowledge, experience and contacts, having worked as Sol Kersner's PR lady. (Sol, attained South African and International acclaim with his Southern Sun hotels, notably Sun City, and then moved on to the Atlantis in the Bahamas, where Melanie last worked for him.)

Melanie was a petite blond and a seasoned PR lady. She had an ageless charm about her. We talked a lot, and I even learned that we had common friends, like Gert Grobler, a South African diplomat who was once stationed in London.

In Ramallah, Melanie immediately got down to work, meeting with several PR companies, accompanied by Maysoun. Eventually she selected SKY, owned by Tariq, the son of President Abbas. On the Israeli-side Melanie also visited many PR companies, and eventually she chose Gitam Porter Novelli. With these two local PR companies lined up, we were ready for the launch of 93.6 RAM FM.

Gitam Porter Novelli arranged a communication and television work-shop and training session at the American Colony hotel for Issie, Maysoun, Andrew, and Keith prior to the launch. Their attention to detail and profes-sionalism was beginning to show. The efforts of SKY paled in comparison. On the other hand, SKY worked under the Israeli occupation.

On meeting Melanie for the first time, what intrigued me most about

Raf, Kevin, Mark, Andrew, and John in Ramallah

her was her reaction when she saw a picture of the late Yasser Arafat with Maysoun and me, We hung this photo strategically in Maysoun's Ramallah office. It was meant to send a message to junior officials from the various Palestinian ministries, who made regular forays to our offices. They often tried to intimidate us or to solicit something in return for doing their jobs. They were suspicious and were stretching to fit our work into a conspiracy theory. When they faced our photo with Arafat, they got the message that we were "connected," and that they ought to let us be.

Melanie, however, reacted differently. She shrieked and closed her eyes to avoid looking at Arafat. "He is the devil incarnate," she blurted. In that instance, I could see how propaganda works. To Palestinians the picture said one thing. Yet, to a South African Jewess it said something entirely different. I could never ever have imagined her response. One person's freedom fighter is another's terrorist. Mandela spoke about this, and I had come to a similar conclusion in a philosophical way. Now, I saw that in practical down-to-earth terms: we had our work cut out.

As the Jerusalem studios were still under construction, Issie and the team made a decision to go ahead and launch the station from Ramallah, which was the correct thing to do, as our license was issued by the Palestinians.

At 6 am, 21 February 2007 on a cold and wet winter's morning, John Berks launched 93.6 RAM FM with the John Lennon song, "Give Peace a Chance."

In doing so, he preferred his choice over the John Mayer song, "Waiting on the World to Change," a hit song at the time. Our music manager, Peter Tarnawski, felt strongly that the John Mayer tune was the most appropriate.

John's failure to consider the wishes of Peter, set the scene for a major clash between him and the Aussies, whom he detested with a passion. John never forgave an Aussie consultant who, in his South African days, recommended Primedia to have him replaced with Gareth Cliff on Radio 702.

John came in early that morning from Jerusalem via taxi, courtesy of Dawood, our friend who drove and personally witnessed the building of RAM FM. John, even commented on air, about driving through potholes and puddles of water through the Kalandia Checkpoint, which Palestinians were subject to daily.

Melanie's scored huge triumph: the launch went live on CNN with Ben Wedeman. And Wedeman marveled out loud at our radio project, as the world watched and listened.

In a humble studio with offices in Ramallah, a South African initiative was born. It brought our own experience from South Africa into a conflict between Semitic cousins. It not only gave me a lovely feeling but made me believe that this was the beginning of something truly amazing. When Ben spoke to me, I likened my feeling to that expressed by the leader of the "A Team" (the popular television series) whenever a plan came together. Off camera, I told Ben, "We traversed a difficult road to get here. Yet, it was all worth it."

With the hive of activity around the offices and within the studio, all that mattered to me was that we were finally broadcasting.

Prior to the official launch, Issie brought on board, another South African in Candice Evrard, to handle sales and marketing on the Israeli side. And I was asked to do the same on the Palestinian side. My role as consultant expanded. I was underpaid, which was fine by me. The project and its success meant more to me than the financial rewards. Soon I was knocking on the doors of leading companies in Palestine, selling them RAM FM—a drastic change from my days as ambassador.

Issie drew on his success with Radio 702 in Johannesburg, whereby on obtaining the license, he gathered all the large advertising houses and offered them a deal they simply couldn't refuse. He firmly believed that one should give to receive. He offered them three months of advertising for free with no obligations. On the second month they had to choose either to continue or not. If they did continue, they would be billed at the market rate for a yearly contract. If they did not wish to continue, they would be given the 3rd month for free, and they could then leave with no hard feelings. I believed it was a fair deal and I accordingly sold the same to Palestinians representing multi-national companies.

Candice, was a South African Jewess, who was "making Aliyah"—meaning she was returning to the Jewish homeland to settle for good. She felt it unwise to visit Ramallah, as it would not be looked upon favorably by her handlers in Jerusalem. They were subjecting her to the usual Israeli narrative and propaganda. I insisted that "product knowledge" was the key to marketing and selling. But she remained adamant, and it showed, since she failed to bring a single advertiser on board.

On the day of the launch, I had Coke, Western Union (international brands) and Dallah Rent a Car (Jerusalem based company with offices in Ramallah) on board, providing the station a semblance of a commercial sound.

Tyson Herbeger, an American Jew, who also made "Aliyah" like Candice, had absolutely no issues about visiting Ramallah, which he often did. Tyson joined our news team and absolutely believed in our mission, which was like a breath of fresh air. Tyson even hosted the entire team at his home in Jerusalem for a Sabbath dinner.

Back to the launch: John desired from the beginning to have a co-host and we asked our receptionist Ibtisam Rashid, a petite American Palestinian with a lovely voice and who looked like Chrissie Hynde of the Pretenders, to sit-in. Everyone called her Suma, and she had an infectious sense of humor with a hearty laugh. She was the perfect foil for John, who lapped it up. They were ably assisted by Francis Battika, a youthful Palestinian who was passionate about sound and IT. He operated the panel and phone lines for John as well as played the music.

Watching a South African Jew, an American Palestinian, and a Christian Palestinian working together in a Ramallah radio studio and having loads of fun, was indeed a sight to behold, and CNN captured this historic moment and beamed it across the world. Was this the birth of hope in this land of conflict and wars?

Andrew and his news team, provided full-bulletins on the top of the hour and summaries at the bottom, with stringers and sound bites adding a professional touch to Middle East Eyewitness News. Our news bulletins announced, "in touch, in tune and independent."

After the successful launch in Ramallah, I drove Maysoun, the station manager, and Andrew, the head of our news team, to Tel Aviv, to team up with Issie and Keith, for the official media launch of RAM FM.

Melanie staged the launch at the premises of the Foreign Press Association and invited both the local, as well as the foreign media. The place was packed. Issie was beaming with joy, as his project had finally taken off. He was accompanied on stage by Maysoun, his trusted lieutenant, Keith, and Andrew.

We launched RAM FM with a message recorded and played from Nelson Mandela. "Keep the nation talking." Mandela spoke, "For they say it is when the talking starts that the fighting stops."

Issie's message was similar. "What we are aiming for," Issie said, "is ultimately to be a talk station to enable Israelis and Palestinians to phone in and talk about issues that affect their lives, to set aside misconceptions, to set aside fears and to try and build confidence. If people don't talk to each other, this to me is the biggest issue between Israelis and Palestinians: that at grassroots level there is no trust."

Issie called the venture a leap of faith and noted that it was based on hardheaded business sense and market research, which showed that RAM FM had strong potential to attract a target audience of 500,000 English speakers—60% of Israelis and 40% of Palestinians between the ages of eighteen and forty-nine.

Some compared our project to Abie Nathan's "voice of peace." (This was a radio station that once broadcast from a ship "somewhere in the Mediterranean.")

Issie responded. "We're not taking off after Abie," he said. "I think he had a noble cause . . . but he's also construed as a pirate. We're not pirates. But I do admire his initiative. I think he had guts, and it is just a pity that he didn't achieve what he intended to do."

"With studios in Ramallah and Jerusalem," Izzie added, "RAM FM, aspires to act as a platform for peace and dialogue, based on a successful Johannesburg station, Radio 702."

Radio 702 was founded during the height of apartheid. Its talk show format, combined with music and news, was a new phenomenon. Over time its freewheeling nature and openness developed broke down the compartments that Apartheid had created. People could break out and talk to each other, although the apartheid regime tried its best to prevent this discourse. 702 made possible people-to-people contact.

Now, more than a quarter-century later, Issie, Maysoun, me and Issie's business partners, created an ambitious project to bring to the Israeli-Palestinian conflict. The objectives were similar: to provide an open, robust forum in which ordinary Israelis, Palestinians and others could interact and express their views in a way the bitter political conflict normally prevented. Programming would include music, talk and news.

There was something different about this enterprise because of radio's ability to reach a large listenership across borders in real-time. It can access people in every corner of society in ways other media cannot do. Masses of people can participate—passively or actively—from homes, businesses, schools or wherever else they happen to be, without having to be formally part of a dialogue project. They can call in or just listen to the debate while doing other things.

If people can talk to each other—even if they vehemently disagree—it encourages them to see the other as more human and maybe even find some commonality. High-level talks between the two sides have always been—and continue to be—held, openly or in secret. What these have lacked is the involvement of the person-in-the-street in being prepared to talk to those on the other side.

Andrew added: "News coverage would be independent, accurate and use neither of the terms terrorist or martyr. We are committed to telling both sides of the story. We are apolitical and will not tow any political line, other than peace. English is a neutral language; the language of mediation and it is used in international peace talks and it shows that we are not taking a particular side."

Thereafter, Maysoun, Keith and Andrew ably answered all the questions posed by the large international media contingent who were excited about some good news in a land of eternal conflict.

After a most successful press conference in Tel Aviv, we all headed back to Ramallah to do the same at a venue adjoining Darna restaurant, which was teaming with local and regional Arab media, as well as some foreign journalists based in Palestine.

The same followed in Ramallah but mostly it placed the project in its proper context and put to rest the various conspiracy theories that were gaining currency in town, as Issie was most forthright in outlining his vision and intentions for RAM FM, which was "to broadcast entertainment, music and informative programs which will promote peace and dialogue and provide reliable, impartial and independent news from the Middle East."

We then headed back to the studios/offices of RAM FM and I recall Issie sitting in Maysoun's office, being interviewed by an Israeli reporter from the daily, *Ma'ariv* and in all humility, he looked at Maysoun and me, and attributed the success to us, especially to Maysoun.

By this time, some were saying, "RAM FM means Raf and Maysoun FM." We had to dispel this quickly so that it did not gain any currency. Another one was, "RAM FM means, Raf, Adam, Maysoun FM."

Most of all, the hype that the launch and the two press conferences created lasted for quite a while, as we were inundated with visits by media from across the region and globe.

We had announced that RAM FM was on air and everyone took note of our presence and we went on to receive voluminous coverage from as far as Japan and Mexico—a South African initiative that sought to create a platform for entertainment, dialogue and hopefully usher in peace in the Holy Land of conflict.

The evening of the launch, Dave Harden from USAID, scheduled a meeting with Maysoun and myself at the American Colony hotel. Dave asked probing questions to which we provided forthright answers, which led to him writing detailed notes. Having been a diplomat myself, I understood that he was reporting a major peace initiative to his principles, and in a sense, we obtained comfort that the Americans, the key player in the conflict, knew all about us. It kind of provided us with a safety net, is what I surmised.

Within the week, the Jerusalem studios were completed, and John's breakfast show relocated there. In Jerusalem, he was ably assisted by Andrew and his news team of Tyson and Ashira Ramadan.

The Ramallah studio was designed in a way to accommodate the presenter and guests, with the adjoining room serving for news bulletins and seating the producer who placed and took phone calls from interviewees and the audience. The configuration came from Primedia and we implemented it accordingly. It was a functional studio with amazing sound proofing that created lovely acoustics. On the other hand, the Jerusalem studio was specifically designed for John, who sat in one room with his guest/s while the panel and operator sat in another, as John was not interested to learn how to use the panel and all the IT related equipment, guess he was still lost in time.

With the Jerusalem studios on the 11th floor, the windows provided a panoramic view of the surroundings and sound proofing was somewhat limited, totally different from Ramallah. And with the crisp newness and colorful décor of the studios, it was no wonder the atmosphere felt as breezy as the music that was broadcast from there.

Since there was a short time-delay between the two studios, a direct camera link in real time was installed. This meant that we saw one another and when the switch over for news and programming took place, we could indicate with a thumbs-up sign.

The breakfast and morning shows came from Jerusalem and the afternoon and drive shows from Ramallah. We played only English language contemporary global music, with hourly news bulletins from 6 am to 7 pm Sunday to Thursday and one detailed news bulletin on Fridays and Saturdays at 1 pm.

At night, we switched onto automation and played music.

The next stage was to introduce talk shows and high-profile interviews as well as night time shows.

As for the Breakfast Show and much to John's disappointment, he could not have Suma in Jerusalem as she was barred to travel there, being a Palestinian from the West Bank. Nevertheless, he tried in vain with two American Jewesses. He simply wanted a woman as a sounding board and not someone who had her own mind and personality. The Americans wanted to be more assertive. John had a hard time adapting from a formula that had worked in South African but was not going to work in this more modern world in the Holy Lands.

We then had to shelve the idea of a morning show co-host for John. He settled for a show with his panel man, Francis and they made an effective team, although they often had issues—such is the nature of show business and its egos.

Following on the heels of the Breakfast show, Mike Brand a British Jew who made "Aliyah" did the morning show from Jerusalem, from 9 to 12. After him, Hayat Alami, a Palestinian, hosted the show from 12 to 3, in Ramallah. Both had been recruited by the Australian consultant Peter Butler. Mike had worked previously for Abe Nathan's Peace Radio which broadcast from a ship in the Mediterranean and was closed by the Israelis, and Hayat's claim to fame was her work for IPCRI, a Palestinian/Israeli Peace NGO.

After the Israeli and Palestinian, we had Barry Hill, who hailed from Newcastle in Australia, with years of radio experience under his belt, and who came across as a typical Aussie bloke one could sit down with at a pub and over a drink engage in a chat. Barry did the drive show from 3 to 6 and his was a smooth no-nonsense music show which most listeners, on both sides of the divide, loved.

On weekends, Peter Tarnawski came up with a novel idea. He lined up potential DJs, trained them on the use of the panel, provided them with music and air-time. Peter then listened and evaluated their performances. In this way he discovered talent that we could further develop.

It was through this method that we discovered Arda Aghazarian. She was the most hardworking of the whole lot of potential DJs. One afternoon while we were traveling between Jerusalem and Ramallah listening to RAM FM, she played the song, "Save the last dance for me," by Michael Bublé (a song that tells the story of a couple at a dance). Arda, at the end of the song, explained that the composer of the song tells his wife that she is free to dance and socialize with other men throughout the evening, but she should not forget that she is going home with him.

The songwriting team of Doc Pomus and Mort Shuman, as Arda explained, wrote this song and their inspiration for the song came from a very personal experience. One night, Pomus found a wedding invitation in a hatbox. Back came his most vivid memory from his wedding: watching his brother Raoul dance with his new wife while Doc, who had polio, sat in his wheelchair.

On hearing this, Peter and our team were so touched and impressed by Arda that she was immediately brought on board. Soon she blossomed with RAM FM.

The morning news came from Jerusalem and was led by Andrew and his team of Tyson and Ashira. They were joined by stringers from around the region, from Beirut to the Gaza Strip, adding in segments and sound bites.

After midday, however, the news was read from Ramallah where Mark Klusener headed a team comprising of Abdullah Erekat, an American Palestinian, and Shireen Yassin, a Palestinian from the old city of Jerusalem. Our news was without any editorial comment, meaning that the facts were reported by both by the reader and the stringer. Afterward, editorial comment was offered by both sides. For example if an Israeli airstrike took place against a Hamas target in Gaza, our news reader would begin with the story and then cross over to our correspondent in Gaza, Ashraf Shannon, who would provide the facts only. Then we would obtain comment from both the Israeli and Hamas sides. This was factual and impartial news in a conflict zone and our listeners loved it.

Every morning, Andrew would also read the headlines from the two Israeli English language newspapers, *Jerusalem Post* and *Haaretz*. To be fair and balanced, Andrew would translate into English the headlines from the Arabic newspaper, *Al Quds* and read it, as there was no English newspaper on the Palestinian side.

For this, Marwan, one of the owners of *Al Quds,* who soon became a huge fan of the station, provided us lots of free advertising and coverage. We also obtained regular coverage from the Israeli dailies through the sterling efforts of our PR Company, Gitam Porter Novelli.

And with radio we often broke stories. The best compliment we received was from Ben Wedeman of CNN. "I listen to your news bulletins all the time," He said, "to pick up on stories that need to be developed for TV." All-in-all, RAM FM was up and running, providing great music and news bulletins. Still, the talk shows were not functioning, and listeners were not phoning in.

John, with years of experience in South Africa, was pretty much naive about Palestine and Israel. Although he made an effort, every time he ended up sticking his foot in. One morning he posed the question on air, "All those who have come to live here, like me," he said, "call me and let's talk about the trials and tribulations of settling in."

Immediately I called him and asked him to drop it and not to take any callers whatsoever. He expressed an initial reluctance. Then, I had to explain to him that our license was granted by the Palestinians. I made him understand the reality: Any Jew from anywhere in the world was free to come to Israel and settle here on land that Palestinian's claim as belonging to them. The creation of the state of Israel led to Palestinian displacement. Some writers simply say, "Palestinians were ethnically cleansed from their own land." This was a reality and something that was at the core of the conflict and hurtful to Palestinians. Now, imagine a whole bunch of Israeli settlers calling in on a Palestinian licensed radio station and talking to a South African Jew about settling here.

John got the message. From that point on, he refrained from politically sensitive issues. Instead he stuck with topics like, "spare the rod and spoil the child" and other human-interest subjects, which somehow found resonance with both audiences. He did not understand the "lay of the land." These were the words uttered to me by an Israeli security official at the airport in Johannesburg, prior to a flight I was taking after attending proceedings related to my court case against the department of foreign affairs. He told me all about myself as he searched my luggage. This is the norm for non-Jews traveling to Israel from anywhere in the world.

Meanwhile John continued having issues with the Aussies at the station, especially with Peter who sought to impose "the Australian way," which was strict and regimented according to John. In John's view, it gave Peter power over the presenters, whereas John refused to play by the rules of others. He was a rule unto himself—always behaving like a diva!

The clash got so bad, that John eventually complained to Issie that Peter was anti-Semitic. Peter had no answer and so he left. Peter meant well and tried hard in the time he was here.

Peter was then replaced by Kevin Lee (Oberstein) from Johannesburg who gained much fame as a DJ but with a romance gone sour, he landed up in a rehabilitation center where he was recovering from alcohol and drug addiction. Issie gave Kevin a second chance and Maysoun and I took personal care of him. He moved into an apartment in Ramallah and according to his contract he was to see a therapist and do regular blood tests. Soon, his passion for music healed him.

Kevin was a workaholic and spent hours in our studios, taking the music of the station from the staid Aussie sound to an internationally acclaimed one. We even received emails from New York, with listeners stating they preferred listening to RAM FM via streaming than any local station.

Mike Brand, on the other hand, tried the people-to-people thing and interviewed both Palestinians and Israelis on his show, on non-political issues. This was audience outreach, but it was hampered by Mike's bland and non-engaging style. Mike made clear that he felt he was more talented than John, which drubbed many in his audience the wrong way.

Dr Sabri Saidam, the Palestinian telecommunications minister who issued us the license, became an avid fan of the station, and after a cabinet reshuffle, went back to academia. He was an ideal guest for our station. Maysoun obtained a permit for him from the Israeli army offices adjacent to Ramallah, and I drove him to Jerusalem, bragging about our project on the way and thanking him for his role in helping to make it happen. He was scheduled to be hosted on Mike's show and to talk about technology in Palestine, with an emphasis on how it may be used to bridge the divide.

Mike had two written questions, which he read out at the beginning of the interview. Once Sabri had answered them, the interview was over. "Why," I wondered, "did Maysoun and I go to all this work for five minutes of live radio?"

Mike's interviewing skills were wanting, to say the least. I tried to address this during a scheduled talk, assisted by Andrew, but Mike's ego was much bigger than our vision and he was not going to change.

Meanwhile John energetically engaged in building an audience for RAM FM. Without a doubt he brought on-board ex-South Africans now living in Israel, fans of his from his LM Radio, Capital Radio, and Radio 702 days. He was especially appealing to those living in Ranana. With very few on-air callers, however, we had no idea about the demographics or the spread of the audience, until one morning when I arrived at the studios in Jerusalem.

Maysoun had designed golf shirts with the station's logo for the presenters and staff to wear and I took along John's, whilst sporting my own. John, who was on-air, immediately went on a rave about the shirt I was wearing and then asked listeners to call the studio, and the first three callers would receive free golf shirts with the RAM FM logo. That did it!

Suddenly, the lines were jammed and John was in his element—talking to as many listeners as possible and asking them where they were calling from, how they had learned about RAM FM, and what they liked most about the station. This interaction was most informative to all of us and it set a trend for competitions and prizes on all our shows, with added interaction between presenter and listener.

From that day, we gave away T-shirts, coffee cups, caps, bags and jumpers all with 93.6 RAM FM logos. On the streets, we often came across listeners sporting with our swag, on both sides of the divide.

Meanwhile the international media continued focusing on our radio project. Not a week went by without us being visited by journalists or camera crews. Apparently, our story was now considered "sexy" . . . the prevailing flavor of the year. Locally, however, we were not gaining traction.

Our aim was to build an audience. It didn't take much convincing from our Israeli PR company for Issie to splurge on two billboards on the Ayalon Freeway in Tel Aviv. These huge ads announced our existence, and that led many Israeli radio enthusiasts switching their dials to RAM FM on their daily commute. We followed up on the Palestinian side as well, with billboards on the Jerusalem to Ramallah via Kalandia route, obtaining the same results.

Up to this stage, I basically played a role from the side-lines, advising and assisting whenever the need arose and constantly doing the PR, marketing and selling.

I worked closely with Issie to try to bring companies and commercials on board. Radio 702 was licensed in the apartheid homeland of Bophuthatswana and featured commercials from South Africa. Izzie felt that he could do the same with RAM FM.

Most consumer products came from Israel into the Palestinian market, and Israeli advertisers relished the radio advertising opportunity. However Palestinian radio license regulations, and especially the ministries concerned, forbade airing of Israeli commercials. So, the successful South African Radio 702 model could not be replicated.

Sufficient funding was raised by Issie and his shareholders for the radio station to operate for one year with no income. Yet we needed to be making money in twelve months. Given the status of Israeli/Palestinian political relations, there was no likelihood of any advertising income from either side.

So, Issie and I devised three out-of-the-box potential income earning opportunities:
- To approach thirty major global companies through their corporate social investment programs to support the project, on the premise that they believe in the concept of peace in the Middle East and could enhance their brand image in the process.
- To set-up subscription-based Internet streaming
- To establish a syndicated English network of radio stations (one per city) globally, providing each with exclusive access to the station's news and special programs. Delivery either by satellite or Internet.

We tried to obtain multinational brands, but then collided with another issue. Palestinians believed that their market was in the Arabic media. Furthermore they did not have the budgets to invest in RAM FM commercials, as our prices were determined by the market rate in Tel Aviv, whereas local Arabic radio was dirt cheap by comparison.

On the Israeli side, companies representing multinational brands were keen to advertise but not the generic brand as that would be counterproductive to their marketing and sales campaigns.

With this dilemma Issie then opted for Plan B. (I loved his never-give-up approach.) So Issie and I headed to Dubai to meet with regional heads of multinational brands. In Dubai, we spent a week selling RAM FM—in the same city where I served as South Africa's ambassador for three years.

Most people bought into our sales pitch. Good. However, their agents in Palestine and Israel had to go along with it. They did not, for example, dialogue with the leaders whom we convinced in Dubai. Instead, they referred the decision to their agent in Bethlehem. Now we heard that our rates were too expensive. Catch 22.

I then met with the newly appointed minister of information in Palestine, Dr Mustapha Barghouti whose acquaintance I had made during my sojourn as the ambassador, and once again ran into a wall. "No Israeli ads, period!" said Barghouti.

Issie, undeterred, followed through with Plan C. He flew to the United States, to meet with heads of multinationals there to try and secure funding from their CSO (Civil Society Organization) budgets. He did not get very far, because we were a commercial entity and not an NGO.

Had we taken the NGO route, funding was in the offing, but as a businessman, Issie believed RAM FM had the potential to make money as he had done with Radio 702 in the apartheid homeland of Bophuthatswana.

Meanwhile the show went on, as Palestinians and Israelis loved the music that RAM FM played, and our news bulletins obtained a faithful following on both sides of the divide. The talk shows, however, were dead, the commercials were not being sold. Still, Issie continued pouring in his own money.

4 Return to Radio

20 years later—from an Ambassador to a DJ/Talk Radio Host

A ND THEN I MADE MY COMEBACK, marrying the two loves of my life—diplomacy and media.

Mike Brand had to take a day off, as it was a Jewish holiday, I put up my hand to stand in for him and do the morning show from 9 to 12.

Twenty years ago, I did my last show on Radio Lotus in South Africa, from a studio in Pretoria, where I counted down the top 10 hits of the week, beginning with Sandra's, "Hi!" And ending it with Europe's, "The Final Countdown." Much had changed since. The days of vinyl records and reels of tape were a thing of the past. Radio had made strides with the advent of computer technology coupled with countless advantages. So, the day before, I received intensive training on how to operate the mixer, board and all the computer paraphernalia that goes with today's on air broadcasting.

Mike's show featured "Classic 9@9," a copy from an Australian radio program in Sydney—introduced by Peter—whereby Mike played nine classic songs with a theme, like nine songs by British artists and so on. It was nice but flat and he followed up with boring interviews.

True to my nature, I creatively added the element of a competition to "Classic 9@9" and on that very first morning, from the studios in Ramallah, I made a dramatic comeback in my unique style. And this is how it all panned out. . . .

Andrew read the 9 am news from the Jerusalem studios. We had a link up, whereby we could see one another on computer screens from studios in either city. This was necessary as there was a slight delay in the cross-over, caused by the micro-wave link between Ramallah and Jerusalem, and therefore the on air presenter would make a manual switch on Andrew's thumbs up sign, once he had read his last word from the news bulletin.

On cue, I played the popular song at the time: "Who Let the Dogs Out." I watched on my screen, Andrew and Francis, his panel man, crack themselves up with laughter and then at the opportune moment, during a music-only part of the song, I introduced myself and the competition and did it with my last word succeeded by the first word at the beginning of the vocals of the song—a skill I honed to perfection at Radio Lotus and twenty years later, I introduced my signature style to a brand-new audience.

Thereafter, I played nine songs related to animals: "Buffalo Soldier," "Crocodile Rock," and seven others, and then had the phone lines jammed with callers lined-up on the last song. The first caller with the correct answer won a RAM FM T-shirt.

This was lots of fun and games to begin with, which introduced another dimension to RAM FM. And so the lifeless morning show was resuscitated and given a new lease on life.

Then it was time for "Talk @10." I brought into the studio the mayor of Ramallah, Ms Janet, a Christian woman who was appointed by the Hamas government that had recently won the elections—a surprise for our Israeli listeners who did not know this fact. We then spoke about her life, her work and the challenges she faced and especially how she went about surmounting them. Janet was relaxed, articulate and once again I added another of my signature styles from Radio Lotus, playing music in-between the chatting, so as not to switch-off the music listeners with too much talk.

I had so much fun doing this show, and like all good things time soon ran out. With my adrenaline on a high, I left the studio to positive acknowledgment from my colleagues, who had listened intently. Before I could settle down, we received a most complimentary email from Shannon Fahey in Sydney, whom Issie employed as a consultant to monitor and improve programming, after she had achieved much success with "Cape Talk" in Cape Town. She had listened on the Internet to both my shows and insisted that I immediately take over from Mike, who was going nowhere with the morning show. She liked the freshness I added to "Classic 9@9" and loved the smooth style I brought to "Talk @10."

In a later email of October 8, 2007 Shannon wrote to Maysoun, "I am very happy with the level of Raf's interviews. This is the show that needs the least amount of "work" and attention! It just ticks along . . . he is getting the high-level guests and just letting it flow. His interview technique has come along, and he is finding his way with it all. A very respectful interviewer for very complicated and serious material . . . today was essentially a political analysis of the current political process with a political scientist. Quite heavy stuff. . . and yet it totally works on the station with him as interviewer. If it was anyone else at this stage . . . I don't think this would fit to be honest Maysoun. In his second last link. He did a good wrap up of the show . . . now in the last link . . . excellent closer . . . Great stuff. Very good. He is sounding great."

Returning to radio, was yet another journey with RAM FM—I started solely as an advisor, then became a political consultant, and progressed to joining Issie in PR, marketing and selling the station, and on that fateful day, I put up my hand to host the morning show and not only enjoyed doing it, but I was just what Shannon was looking for—a person who could handle both sides of the story in a neutral and sensitive manner.

Issie initially expressed skepticism, noting that I would no longer be answerable to him but "Maysoun would be your boss." She was previously my assistant when I was an ambassador—reversal of roles compounded by the fact that we were married. This didn't matter to me, as the idea and vision of RAM FM was larger than both my manhood and ego.

I then made the transition from being the South African ambassador to the Palestinian national authority, a VIP, where I would visit, inform, and protest on what was happening to Palestinians only, to become the host of the sole political talk show that provided a platform for both Palestinians and Israelis in English. It was then time for me to engage Israeli society, understand its fears and problems, to have a comprehensive picture of the conflict, and I began on a new career that married diplomacy, music and communication, which I believed my life's journey had prepared me for—to provide a platform and build bridges of understanding between Semitic cousins embroiled in an intractable conflict.

"Classic 9@9" posed a daily challenge—I had to find a new set of nine songs with a common thread or theme, which I somehow managed to do. Some were relatively easy, like nine songs by female artists, whereas others were not and one that the audience failed to figure out was nine songs that began with the titles of the songs.

Every morning, I spoke to John Berks at the end of his show, as he handed over the baton to me. If I was in Ramallah, we would do this by phone, but if I was in Jerusalem, I would walk into the studio and do it face to face. He would ask me about the "Classic 9@9" and I would provide clues, the beginning of fun and games for the morning. With the Internet and emails, we learned that there was a huge fan club of avid listeners glued to their radios as they waited each morning, even enjoying the music I featured on this show.

For Israeli listeners traveling on the congested highways "Classic 9@9" was a welcome distraction from the delays caused by traffic and for Palestinians sitting at checkpoints, it provided a welcome relief.

Then there was the part, where we encouraged winners to come in, either to the Jerusalem or Ramallah studios to pick up their prizes, which lent us to get to know our audience better.

Before I cite one such occasion, let me explain why I did my shows from both Jerusalem and Ramallah, whereas all the other presenters were based in just one of them. As a South African, I could cross-over and work from both Jerusalem and Ramallah and more so because I desired to do so. On days that my studio guest/s was in Ramallah, I would do my show from there and on days when they were in Jerusalem I would travel there.

Following from "Classic 9@9" was "Talk @10," which provided a platform for Israelis and Palestinians to be spoken to by the other, via phone calls on the talk shows—something never done before!

The Ramallah studio was sealed off on all sides with heavy insulation material, and although it produced a wonderful sound, it made one feel as if one was in a prison, whereas the Jerusalem studio, perched on the 11th floor and overlooking the beautiful mountainous terrain of the western part of the city, was the complete opposite and it had this sense of being free. For me, this also manifested the difference between the two sides.

Getting back to that occasion—two ranked Israeli soldiers won prizes on "Classic 9@9" and came along to the Jerusalem studio to not only pick up their prizes, but to meet with Raf, whom they perceived as a rocking DJ. Our secretary was surprised when they entered, dressed in their military uniforms with guns slung over their shoulders. I had just stepped out of the studio during a music break and was equally surprised to see them. When one of them said, "Where is Raf? We have come to see him . . . Raf rocks!" That did it.

I stepped up and introduced myself, to their utter surprise. They did not expect me to 'look' like a Palestinian, but seizing the moment, I began talking a common language and asked them, "What music you guys enjoy, from which era, 70s, 80s, 90s or current?" and they both said, "80s" and at that point all was forgotten—that I looked like the enemy and they were soldiers, as the bond of music does transcend physical differences.

They then joined me in the studio, seated beside me, as they enjoyed the music and the rest of my show, watching me in action, as I worked the panel and the computer screens with music, jingles and the works—like a professional DJ.

Chatting to listeners, both Israelis and Palestinians on air and via the stacks of emails I received daily, made me realize that music was indeed a bridge and it certainly had no boundaries, in fact it united rather than divided.

Also, on many occasions I would encounter Israeli soldiers manning West Bank checkpoints who would request identification documents from me, and once I opened my mouth, they would realize who I was and call the others to come see me—they acted like groupies, to say the least.

Our excellent signal in the West Bank obtained many Israeli soldiers as avid fans and once a foreign journalist informed me that the DCO, or headquarters of the Israeli army offices just outside of Ramallah blared the music of RAM FM.

And then, on the American fourth of July celebrations at the American Consulate in Jerusalem that Maysoun and I attended, to my surprise, the deputy ambassador from Tel Aviv and his wife 'found' me to tell me that most of the embassy staff listened to my morning show and they really enjoyed it. Now that was some affirmation!

On "Classic 9@9" we gave away, T-shirts, coffee cups, caps, sweatshirts and bags with the station's logo and 'on-air' participation was massive on the Israeli side, but somewhat limited on the Palestinian side—which we tried to figure out and surmised that radio competitions and participation culture was a new phenomenon, that still had to grow, although we did have some contestants and even occasionally from Gaza, which was promising.

All in all, "Classic 9@9" was a highly successful program with a huge and participatory audience.

"Talk @10" was the only political talk-show in Israel and Palestine, which I hosted on the premise: your enemy is a person whose story you have not heard—it provided a platform for all narratives to be aired. The only restriction to free-speech was, I drew the line on hate-speech and incitement, but everything else was either kosher or halal.

I was also grounded in this reality—knowing that the Israeli-Palestinian conflict was vastly more complex—and, in many ways, more intractable—than South Africa's apartheid struggle. The violent religious zealots who riddle the middle east will not easily be influenced—and may view RAM FM in a hostile light, since their interest is not in peace-making. Such powerful religious and political elements play a huge role in keeping the conflict burning. The obvious danger was that my talk shows could degenerate into tit-for-tat slanging matches where point-scoring and spewing out of hatred and intransigence became the order of the day, and nobody would be listening to anyone else. I needed the wisdom of Solomon to negotiate this minefield of Mideast politics and to give RAM FM a chance of succeeding, and I was always ready for that challenge.

I hosted guests from the Israeli-left, like Uri Avnery and Gideon Levy to Benny Alon and Caroline Glick on the right of the political spectrum and politicians from Silvan Shalom on the Israeli side to Mustafa Barghouti in Palestine. On the Palestinian side, I had guests from Fatah, Hamas, and those critical of both parties—a wide spectrum of a cross section of both societies graced "Talk @10." Radio and modern communication even enabled me to host guests from all over the world, like Ziggy Marley whom I spoke to in Los Angeles, Israeli Knesset Speaker while she was in Paris and many more.

Some days, I chose topics that divided, like checkpoints which Palestinians hated because they hindered free-movement, but Israelis loved because for them they provided a sense of security. On other days, I chose topics that united, like talking to mothers, both Palestinian and Israeli, who belonged to an organization, 'Bereaved Parents Association', whose members had lost loved ones to the senseless conflict. And then I dealt with neutral issues like reading the future, by hosting a leading Israeli psychic on the show, who would tell listeners on both sides with amazing accuracy their concerns and futures.

Essentially, the political issue of the day, determined whom we interviewed, but we always strove to maintain an objective balance in our choice of guests. I always tried to delve into the story behind the story with the persons making up the story, in a sober and impartial manner. We had the advantage of radio, which is immediate and with telephonic connections on both sides, it gave us the edge, although we generally preferred our guests to come into the studios.

My questioning was always open-ended, allowing my guests to freely express their respective views, and many Israelis informed me that they were particularly pleased with this approach when compared to their own highly confrontational interviewers on their radio stations. "Talk @10" built a huge and attentive audience, evident by the large email traffic commenting on the issues raised. Listeners, who called in, were handled sympathetically and we made sure that they were given a platform to express their views, regardless of where they stood on the political spectrum. In short, I facilitated this process as a seasoned diplomat that I was and ended up, humanizing people, instead of labeling them according to their political standpoints.

On Thursdays, I did a program called, "The Week That Was." This show hosted leading journalists—international, local, and one from our news team—to look-back and talk about their stories of the week. I probed to bring out fresh insights. This proved so popular that we had journalists lining up on their own accord.

I must relate one interesting moment—I was talking to Ben Wedeman of CNN on his week that was, whilst he was doing a CNN story in Sderot—a missile hit the town—whereupon I got him to do an eyewitness report for RAM FM, guess a first for any radio station anywhere.

Most importantly, the podcast of "Talk @10" would be placed on our website at the end of the show, available for download and listening. Monthly we obtained 'hits' in the region of 40,000—which was another measure of its popularity.

Being a seasoned diplomat, au fair with the political issues but constantly reading and researching, gave me an edge and mainly I aired all sides to the story and probably created a better understanding of the other's narrative—in my humble view, the building block to a peaceful resolution of the conflict.

I always believe, there are three sides to every story, mine, yours and the truth which only God knows.

Now let me share with you a normal day of mine. If I was in Ramallah for the day, I would be up before 5 am and immediately get on the Internet to be in step with the news (things changed rapidly in this unfolding drama). Then after a shower and morning tea, I would listen to Andrew's 6 am news, taking cues on the stories we were leading with for the day, sporadically listening to the breakfast show, as I drove to the offices of RAM FM, to be there by 7 am There I would continue with research and preparatory work for my show and then be in the studios from 9 to 12—putting my heart and soul into those three hours, would simply drain me.

After which I would take a small break and then continue with prep for the next day's show as well as do PR, marketing and sales with meetings and travel all over the west bank and even into Israel. My day would end way after 6 pm whereupon I would head home, have dinner, spend some time with my baby, Adam and then continue research for the next day's talk show—the story behind the news—and eventually fall asleep, exhausted at around midnight.

On Fridays, I hosted a show—'Solid Gold Friday' and played the hit music of the past, taking listeners back into a tunnel of time and talking about the era, the song as well as the artist or group. Feedback from the audience was most refreshing as they loved reminiscing about times gone by, with blasts from the past, as I fondly called these songs. This show was for 3 hours, and I enjoyed every minute of it.

Most Saturday's I would be at the station with Kevin, and we would work preparing the material, especially choosing the songs for 'Classic 9&9', for the week to come.

On a lighter note—I should share a memorable day on RAM FM—it all began with the breakfast show presenter, Sara B (Cohen) who had come from 'Cape Talk' to sit-in for John Berks, who traveled to Johannesburg. Sara fell ill in the studio and could not continue. I was driving to Jerusalem and received a call from Maysoun, who informed me about the crisis. Thereafter, I had to drive like a maniac through the morning traffic to get there to take over from Sara. After doing most of the breakfast show, I did my three hours and then drove back to Ramallah while Mike and Arda did the midday show. When I got to Ramallah, I learned that Kevin who did the drive show had to accompany Maysoun on urgent business to Radio Tel Aviv. Then I sat on the drive show. Completing that show, I was informed that Hayat who did the evening show could not make it to Ramallah and obviously I had to do her show as well. Exhausted and late at night, I happened to say, 'You're listening to RAF FM instead of RAM FM' and it was immediately picked up by an avid listener who called in to tell me that I was correct for that day, it was indeed RAF FM.

That was the level of my passion for RAM FM and I even coined a phrase, "I am not a jack of all trades and master of none . . . I am a master of many trades and jack of all."

On RAM FM, mine was a labor of love!

Then there were also many funny moments—John Berks was getting lonely in Jerusalem so Mohammed our office manager, got him a Palestinian bird and I took along the bird in a cage to the studio. We talked 'on-air' about his bird and how she would brighten his dull life in Jerusalem, insinuating that we were referring to a woman (a word that was freely used in the swinging 60's). We had a good chuckle and the audience loved it. Like John always said, 'radio is the theatre of the mind'—we were painting pictures with words.

Although, I received a salary equal to that of Candice, the sales and marketing person, who sat in Jerusalem and never brought a single commercial, I worked more than one job on the radio station and even received less than the breakfast show presenter, but like I said before, my belief and commitment to the mission meant more than any monetary rewards.

Anyway, whatever I earned was simply transferred to my lawyers in South Africa to pay for my drawn-out case against the department of foreign affairs—yet, I was single handedly doing, diplomatically what my government ought to have been proud of, but that wasn't the case.

About the South African representation in both Ramallah and Tel Aviv—knowing that the country's foreign policy was rooted in 'supporting the peace process' they nevertheless kept an arm's length from us, though we were South African with many citizens involved. Unlike other countries that were simply all over us, including ambassador Mark Otte, who was the head of the European Union and responsible for the peace process, as well as the Americans, other Europeans and even the Sri Lankan ambassador in Ramallah.

I then reached out to my fellow South Africans on South Africa's Freedom Day, and began with a telephonic interview with the ambassador in Tel Aviv, Fumanekile Gqiba, an ANC cadre who was a former army chaplain. To put it mildly, he was embarrassing and my fellow South Africans at the radio station, were not only provided with humor but expressed sadness that our representation had sunk to such a low level. Then it was time for the South African in Ramallah, Ted Pikane, another ANC cadre, who felt that by being evasive and non-committal he was being diplomatic, when the subject matter was our Freedom Day—enough said!

Getting back to my work day, if I had to do the show from Jerusalem, I was compelled to leave at about 5 am because of the Kalandia checkpoint and then to navigate the Jerusalem morning traffic, to somehow arrive at the studios in Malcha before my show began at 9 am After the show, I had to then drive back to Ramallah and be subject to a long wait at the checkpoint, and this commuting which I took upon myself to do, was tiring but nevertheless fueled by my passion and commitment which kept driving me on.

In Jerusalem, I have fond memories of guests whom I hosted—from rabbis, sheiks and priests talking about interfaith dialogue to a wide spectrum of Israelis from many walks of life and political views. Likewise, in Ramallah I hosted from the renowned Israeli journalist Amira Hass to government ministers and laypersons. Amira even wrote in one of her newspaper columns that she was given total freedom to express her views—a rare occurrence in this part of the world.

All this talk and interaction with both sides and with all political views, certainly added to my understanding of the complexity of the problem and why the effort we were making was not only imperative but had to continue unabated.

My style was unique, in that I provided a platform and played the role of a facilitator. Let me give you one example to illustrate it—I did a show on what the Palestinians call, 'the apartheid wall' as it discriminates and makes their lives miserable whereas Israelis call it a fence as it protects them from potential suicide bombers, but for my show I called it the barrier and had in the studio an Israeli woman from the organization, 'Machshom Watch' that monitors the checkpoints and assists wherever possible, like with cases involving pregnant Palestinian women wanting to cross to hospitals on the other side. Callers from both sides expressed their opinions and I facilitated a much heated but civilized discussion wherein all narratives were aired, and this was certainly an achievement.

There were many Israelis who monitored every word I uttered and if I faltered, they were quick to contact Issie and lay a complaint. Let me cite one such incident. I was interviewing an American, Steve Sosebee, who many years ago, started a non-profit entity, Palestine Children's Relief Fund, to help children obtain medical care in the USA. Steve, came to the region as a journalist and when he saw innocent children being hurt in the conflict, he set up the organization which has since grown phenomenally.

A Mrs Cohen called and asked him why he hadn't done a similar thing for Israeli children. Steve responded that Israel has some of the best medical facilities available and there was no need for him to replicate it. Guess this thing about neutrality and equal treatment got the better of our Mrs Cohen, who then wrote off an email complaining to Issie that I manifested an anti-Israel bias.

Thanks to ICT technology, the entire discussion was emailed to Issie and the matter was resolved. From that moment onwards, Issie provided me with a free-reign. Anyway, we had a code of conduct meticulously drafted by Issie's lawyers in Johannesburg and which we all adhered to after signing it. We were committed to neutrality—period!

I can labor on about my morning show, consisting of "Classic 9@9" and "Talk @10" but let me conceptually explain the 'bridge' it built. The intention of the bridge was to create understanding of the others' narrative. The bridge, built on music, which has no boundaries, was then reinforced with all narratives placed on it, to create understanding, a key element in the peaceful resolution of the conflict.

During the height of Hamas raining their homemade rockets on southern Israel, I asked my producer to get hold of an Israeli in the firing line of these rockets, to talk to him about his fears and experience.

There was this reluctance, as Palestinians felt that I would be providing air-time to a right-wing settler who may utter statements that could jeopardize our license with the Palestinian authority, but I insisted and prevailed.

Anyway, we had this thirty second delay button on interviews and I always had the option of cutting the person off, if he or she crossed the red-line on hate speech or incitement.

"Good morning and a very warm welcome from 'Talk @10' to Ofer Lieberman, resident of kibbutz Nir Amin. Good morning to you!"

"Good morning, sorry I am the manager of the agriculture."

"Okay! Well, to begin with, Ofer take me through what happens when the sirens go off signaling the approach of these homemade projectiles, they called Kassam rockets. Take us through the whole thing."

"Eh! Let's say that we have the alarm, it's called *sevadom* and then we have fifteen to twenty minutes to take a place to hide but the problem is in kibbutz Nir Amin, we don't shelter in the house, so we have a big problem with this."

"So, you don't have bomb shelters?"

"No! We have, but you know the shelter is far from the house, so you cannot come to the shelter in fifteen minutes, fifteen seconds, sorry!"

"Fifteen seconds! Okay! So, how many rockets have come to your part of northern Gaza?

"Inside the kibbutz, inside the area, it's about one-hundred, but around the kibbutz, is agriculture places, it's about 1,000 rockets in the last six, seven years."

"Have there been any casualties?"

"Eh! No! But we have a lot of damage."

"A lot of damage to property and crops?"

"Yes! Houses and plants"

"Well, living under the constant threats and the fear of rocket fire coming from the Gaza Strip, what has it meant for you personally, Ofer?"

"Look, it's very tough to live like this. I have four daughters, ages fifteen, thirteen, ten and six and you know every time there is an alarm you have to take care of all about the children and to look for them and to know what they are doing in this time, its school or the house and this is big problem because my small daughter gets white and she starts to shake every time she hears the alarm."

"Well Ofer, living on this kibbutz, under these constant threats of this rocket fire coming from the Gaza Strip to this community, you must be working together and helping one another?"

"Yes! Of course, we have strong community, so it helps us, you know to pass this time. You know it's a very nice kibbutz, it come on 1943 and every day, you know the kibbutz is like heaven, really it looks like heaven, but you know every day we have between five to ten time like hell."

"Ofer, now let's wrap it up and let's move on the other side. You are a victim on the Israeli-side of the conflict, what are your thoughts, feelings about the victims on the Gaza-side of the conflict?"

"I have a lot of friends in Gaza that I work with and you know, I make a phone call every day, every two days and I speak with them and I know the suffering that they have from this situation. From my side, I prefer that there is a peace between us, you know, I don't care of the Hamas or Fatah or any Israeli government."

"Ofer, thank you so much for speaking with us and we hope you have a good day."

"Thank you, okay bye, and bye!"

This just proved that the average Israeli and Palestinian sought peace, whereas politicians on both sides fanned flames of hatred and violence to simply stay in power.

In a sense, I believed my role was to humanize people, on both sides, regardless of their political or religious beliefs and this interview proved that it was the right thing to do.

Didn't we South Africans representing ALL parties sit around a table at CODESA and finally resolve the issue of apartheid?

5 93.6 RAM FM
Bridged the divide between Israelis and Palestinians

RAM FM WENT ON TO BUILD A SIZABLE AUDIENCE IN ISRAEL, Palestine and beyond, led by Maysoun, who mothered the RAM FM family and created an unprecedented environment, in which everyone brought passion, commitment and enjoyment to his or her daily work in Ramallah and Jerusalem that Maysoun also tirelessly traversed daily.

Anyone walking into either station, simply marveled at how everyone enjoyed working together and the fun they were all having, playing music and providing entertainment, for people engaged in an intractable conflict.

To Maysoun, it was not about politics. It was rather, an audio tool for dialogue and peace between people in conflict. This is what she told the *Jerusalem Post*, "Other than 'Talk @10' and the daily news, the rest of the stuff is what both Israelis and Palestinians care about—health, celebrity gossip, astrology, movie reviews and of course music. The gimmick of RAM FM, if it can be called that, is that it is entirely in English. Even the songs. I see RAM FM as a microcosm of coexistence and what could be. We have in our team, Israelis, Palestinians, Australians, South Africans, Americans, and British. We all work in harmony—without politics coming between us."

Maysoun was often instrumental in hosting the RAM FM family in Ramallah and Jerusalem for dinners and birthday parties and I sometimes lent a hand with my cooking. On one such occasion at a restaurant in Ramallah, Karen, Noah Rothman's (granddaughter of assassinated Israeli Prime Minister Rabin) co-producer, sent along an Israeli crew to shoot footage for the documentary they were working on. The members of the crew were pleasantly surprised to see the harmony amongst the RAM FM band.

Nevertheless, we still faced two challenges, the signal was weak in Jerusalem. This we attributed to the hilly terrain of Jerusalem and surrounds, as Maysoun and I continuously monitored the signal and reported it to Issie and Sergey, and most importantly there was the issue of lack of commercial traffic to generate income.

On the first count, Sergey, our technical guy, recommended that we obtain a second frequency from the Palestinian authority and with our cultivated contacts in the relevant ministries, we easily obtained 87.7 FM for Jerusalem. We then used our first transmitter, which Sergey rehabilitated and placed it with the original antennae system to face Jerusalem from a premise in Ramallah, with a clear line of sight to contact productions in Malcha where our studios were based. Once 87.7 FM was operational, we plugged this new frequency daily and it resulted in a clearer signal and subsequent increase in listeners.

As for commercial traffic, Mustafa Barghouti was replaced by Riad Malki, whom I knew previously as a journalist, as the Minister of Information. Maysoun and I tried to convince him about the positive role RAM FM was playing and for it to be sustainable we needed commercial traffic. At least, grant us permission to have commercials from Israeli products already in the Palestinian market. He too was adamant, no way!

Meanwhile the programming on RAM FM was different compared to what was dished out by the other radio stations in Israel and Palestine. To begin with, our news bulletin, "Middle East Eyewitness News," with the slogan "in touch, in tune and independent" was most unique, unlike biased news bulletins on both sides of the divide. All the terminology was neutral and objective. To provide an example, if the news reader or reporter had to say Al Aqsa, he/she would add Temple Mount. There were many more, like the Israeli Defense Force (IDF) would simply be referred to as the Israeli army, so as not to offend either side.

And this was the modus operandi of the news team. Let's say an attack took place in Gaza. Our news reader would read out the facts and then cross-over to our reporter in Gaza City who would provide visual pictures with words and then we would go to Israeli and Palestinian spokespersons for comment without any editorializing ourselves. It was the most comprehensive and objective news reporting in the region and we had some of the leading international reporters glued to it, to provide them leads, especially for television. And we even had stringers in Baghdad, Damascus and the entire Middle East covered. All in all, our news bulletins were objective and truly professional.

The news team led by Andrew and Mark, who both lived in a penthouse apartment above us in Ramallah and before Andrew moved out to be in Jerusalem, was a highly professional unit. They were always meeting to discuss issues and then socializing to create comradeship and build a cohesive unit.

But it was not all hunky dory as this incident manifests—Ashira and Shireen opted, on a weekend, to take Andrew and Mark on a tour in the West Bank to show them the reality on the ground. Little did they realize that they were traversing terrain filled with perils. . .

They began with a visit to a settlement community of foreign Jews making a life on the land of a people evacuated, and then on their way to Nablus, they viewed a refugee camp of Palestinians evacuated to make way for settlers. In Nablus, they had a clandestine meeting with members of Islamic Jihad at a hospital in the city. Ashira used the occasion to record comments from the Islamic Jihad fighters to use on the news bulletin the next day and this was a major slip-up. Guess she was taken-in by the whole concept of neutrality and providing all sides a voice. Little did she know, the guys they met were wanted by the Israelis, who were obviously monitoring our news bulletins.

Ashira, on her way home to Jerusalem the next evening, was picked up at the Kalandia checkpoint and then jailed for interrogation. It wasn't long before the Israeli army went into Nablus and killed the Islamic Jihad guys our news team had met with on the weekend. Ashira, on her release, was devastated.

Issie paid for her psychological treatment and it was decided that she work permanently in Jerusalem, so as not to cross checkpoints any longer.

Lessons learned by the news crew, lines were drawn, and enthusiasm was kept in check.

On the other hand, the comradeship of the news team was noteworthy. Tyson Herberger, an American Jew who had settled in Jerusalem and who was studying to be a rabbi was so passionate about the news that on the day Abdullah fell ill, he turned up in Ramallah to stand-in for his mate. Everyone knew the afternoon news came from Ramallah and here was Tyson reading it from there, but he was not concerned in the least. That evening, he even joined the team for a drink and a game of pool at a local pub and Tyson looked Jewish, there was no doubt about it.

I was most impressed with what RAM FM was achieving.

As for John Berks and his "Breakfast Show"—he was not emulating the success of his South African radio experience and he kept blaming the Aussies, especially Peter Tarnawski, for his shortcomings. Truth be told, I was once traveling between meetings with Issie in Jerusalem and we were listening to Berks. Issie commented, "John is sounding flat."

John accused Peter of antisemitism, which was not the case, and Issie bought it—resulting in both Peter Tarnawski's (music manager) and Peter Butler's (radio consultant) contracts terminated before completion. They were paid off, and dispatched to the land down-under.

Issie then brought on board Shannon Fahey, a Sydney based program consultant, who had achieved success with "Cape Talk." Shannon mostly monitored the station via the Internet and made a few visits to discuss the way forward with Maysoun and the presenters. Though she looked much like the Australian actress, Nicole Kidman, Shannon was a consummate professional.

Raf and John in Jerusalem

John's contract came to an end. Issie did not renew it and John left—a wealthy man. He was paid a most handsome salary, his home with all the utilities was paid for, he received additional perks and, yet he was always complaining. That was just Berks, as most who knew him from South Africa, surmised. He was replaced by Sara B (Cohen) who came from "Cape Talk," and she too did not grasp the lay of the land and landed here like the proverbial bull in a china shop. Sara had a substance problem and ended up one evening, letting loose on Maysoun in the presence of the team. A phone call to Issie, saw the back of Sara, as Issie was averse to substance abuse on his radio projects.

Sara was then replaced by Martin B, who hailed from the midlands in the United Kingdom. He was a seasoned radio professional, worked previously in Dubai, and he knowingly kept away from politics and dealt with issues that both sides related to, which endeared him well with his faithful band of listeners. Martin brought much needed energy to the "Breakfast Show."

As for the other shows and rest of the team—after my show the afternoon show was hosted by Mike Brand (Israeli) and Arda (Palestinian), who chatted about issues like food, environment and stuff that related to both audiences. They made the point that RAM FM was not a peace station but one that builds bridges.

I enjoyed talking, either on the phone or in the studio when I was in Jerusalem, to Mike and Arda about their upcoming show, and what they were going to talk about, always learning how much Palestinians and Israelis had in common.

The "Drive Show" was initiated by Barry Hill, who at the end of his contract, opted to return to his family in Australia and Kevin Lee (Oberstein) took over. Kevin was a South African Jew, with extensive radio experience, but an emotional breakdown drove him to substance abuse, which then led him to a rehabilitation center in Johannesburg. We found Kevin through contacts at Primedia. Issie liked him but was concerned about his problem. Anyway, and true to his kind-hearted nature, Issie gave him a second chance, but not without tying him into a contact that stipulated severe penalties should he falter.

We felt the best was for Kevin to come and live in Ramallah, which he did in a nice apartment that was within walking distance to the studios. Kevin and I became very good friends as I helped him make the transition from the rehab center to RAM FM. He spent most of his time at the station and revamped the image and music, taking it to a higher level, which even listeners in New York, who tuned in via the Internet commented most positively on.

Kevin got a new lease on life with RAM FM—he was totally passionate about his job and worked 24/7. He went on to introduce a very popular evening show, "The Love Zone" where both sides called in to dedicate songs to their loved ones, but he hated interviews. One evening when he was forced to do a show for another presenter, called "Medically Speaking," he had to talk to a leading Israeli dentist. Kevin ended up making a laughing stock of himself, by asking silly questions and swore never to do it again.

On Kevin's "Drive Show," he pre-recorded and then introduced a new sound each day to run a competition around it. This was so popular that the lines were often jammed with callers. This proved that both sides sought trivial distractions from the lives they were living, and music and entertainment was just the tonic.

I did two things for him—took him to the Wailing Wall in Jerusalem and advised him to offer a prayer of thanks for having been given a second chance and then I arranged a date for him with a lovely Israeli woman, who was a regular telephonic guest on my show. Dawood drove him to and from his date.

Kevin was the music, imaging and the "Drive Show" presenter and he was simply fabulous.

Let me digress for a moment and talk about the continued interest in our story. Noah, the granddaughter of the slain Israeli Prime Minister Rabin, who attained international fame as the little girl at the funeral, invited me to attend the screening of a documentary she made with her friend Karen, at the Cinematheque in Jerusalem, which was also aired on HBO in the States. It was "To Die in Jerusalem," the story of a Palestinian suicide bomber who killed an Israeli girl in Jerusalem and who could have been her twin sister. Our friendship developed from thereon and they then shot footage of RAM FM wishing to make a documentary, as many international television stations did in some way or another.

Then as part of our promotional efforts, we gave away a bumper sticker that read, "93.6 RAM FM stuck on you." When we took Adam to the zoo near Tel Aviv, the people manning the entrance noticed the sticker and informed us that everyone who worked at the zoo listened to us. When I told John Berks about this the next day, he had a field day with it, insinuating that the animals in Israel even listened to RAM FM—that's how popular we had become.

Andrew, whenever he could, cleverly placed a light-hearted story at the end of his news bulletin and John would pick it up and then add his humorous bit to it. Everyone else, also tried to bring much laughter and fun, which was sorely needed here.

I regularly told many funny stories and played songs around them, for which I received lots of appreciative emails, like this one "Sipho, a South African, was married to Loraine but he was in love with a woman named Clearly. One day, he was walking along a river bank and Loraine fell in and drowned. He then ran along, singing—I then played the song by Jimmy Cliff, "I can see clearly now, Loraine is gone."

What we were doing was certainly opening a myriad of vistas for everyone living here.

Karin Laub from Associated Press, wrote this: March 26, 2008—"At an Israeli army base near Ramallah, where Palestinians apply for entry permits to Israel, soldiers set their dial to RAM FM. The manicurist at an upscale Ramallah beauty parlor said her customers enjoy the station's foreign fare . . . In the Israeli town of Ranana, fifty-three-year-old Amanda Elimelech, who immigrated sixteen years ago from Brighton, England, and still has a little trouble with Hebrew, said the sound remind her of home. Palestinian Niveen Shaheen, twenty-eight, from Ramallah said she tunes in for the 90s music. Both said they're eager to hear the political views of the other side, since they can't meet face to face." Laub went on to write—"Gangat said, in all the gloom and doom here, we bring a lot of joy and happiness with our music and positive attitudes."

All in all, the station grew in popularity both in Israel and Palestine as well as internationally, as we streamed on the Internet. We had daily stories related to the bridge we were building with entertainment (music), information (news) and talk (issues of the day and politics)—which we learned about from the emails, interaction on-air and meeting with Israelis and Palestinians.

While Israel was building walls to separate itself from the Palestinians, we were building bridges to connect them by finding the ties that bind and RAM FM had made a difference. We had established a space in the radio environment of the region with a legion of faithful listeners, whom we referred to as the "RAM FM family."

And before we knew it, we were on air for a year and it was time to celebrate and celebrate we did in style.

We began the day with a telephonic interview with a very pleased Issie Kirsch, who recalled the journey with me, but as always, he gave credit to the team at RAM FM who made it happen and continued to do so, a year later.

Then I spoke to all the staff at RAM FM about their time and experiences at the station. The phone lines were jammed with callers and emails coming in bundles. On that day, we had no doubt how big we had grown.

Later in the day, Andrew and I left for an airport in the north of Tel Aviv as guests of The Israel Project, a right-wing organization, with funding from the US. They had targeted us to expose us to their point of view, and a bird's eye one, too. My appearance at the airport and my name created some concern with security, but when the head of the organization arrived, the matter was settled, and we were soon airborne. It was most interesting to view how small the land mass was and how close-for-comfort the two sides are positioned, but the topography of the Holy Land was spectacular.

After flying over the famed old city of Jerusalem, we headed to Sderot where we landed and were shown the remnants of the rockets fired from Gaza. Then we headed back, taking the coastal route. Andrew and I returned to Jerusalem, to learn that the taxi driver was a huge fan, as he immediately recognized us from our distinct voices and South African accents.

Not long thereafter Andrew left for Australia, something he had committed to do as he obtained citizenship and opted to live in the land down-under. He was replaced by another seasoned journalist Xolani Gwala, a Black South African, with whom I spoke isiZulu, much to the wonder of everyone around us. He moved into an apartment in our building and we became good friends, as he slotted very ably into Andrew's shoes.

By this time, we had won an excellence award from NAB (National Association of Broadcasters) in the United States as well as a prestigious Spanish Award.

July 5, 2007—we obtained exclusive rights for Live Earth Concerts— twenty-four musical performances to raise awareness and concern on global warming. Concerts in seven countries, featuring over one-hundred musical acts, including Madonna, Bon Jovi, Red Hot Chili Peppers, Kanye West and Sheryl Crow. RAM FM provided uninterrupted coverage of the entire concert. Our listeners loved the music.

Brit Awards 2008—we streamed live from London, an event hosted by Ozzy and Sharon Osbourne that featured Kylie Minogue, Rihanna and Paul McCartney amongst others.

The World Charts from November 1, 2007 hosted by Florida based personality Lara Scott, which we featured every Saturday noon to 2 pm.

All in all, RAM FM had assumed an international dimension, unlike no other radio station in the region.

Let me dwell for a moment on how we were generally perceived by both sides. The Palestinian left saw us being involved in a project that normalized the Occupation and the Israeli right saw us as a liberal, peace-making project which did not gel with them.

But all in between simply loved us and that is what mattered, the silent majority.

One year later, it was also time to renew our license with the Palestinian authority and we sent along our office manager, Mohamed, to do the necessary, and to our surprise we were visited by junior officials from the ministry of telecommunications, who refused to renew our license. They claimed that we were creating radiation with our transmitters in Ramallah and they were determined to close us down. We pointed out that it was not the case, and how did they determine this, requesting them to provide us the necessary evidence (readings) so that we may be able to then fix the radiation leaks.

I also inquired, "What about the other radio stations in the city?"

The reply I received floored me, "They are not paying license fees, so we cannot do anything to them."

Immediately I headed to Dr Sabri Saidam, the minister, who had become a regular on my talk shows and loved the station for the positive and peaceful role it was playing. The meeting put paid to any shenanigans the junior officials had hatched, license was renewed, and we could continue doing what we were enjoying.

Meanwhile pressure was being built on Issie, as he had progressed from Plan B to C and D. We were now seized on talking to major companies targeting their corporate social responsibility budgets and I was talking to USAID about advertising their services. USAID were sold, save for the fact that we were not an NGO but a commercial radio station.

Creatively we were continuously seeking ways to make RAM FM not only sustainable but economically viable.

Issie continued to finance the running costs with his own funds. Then he brought in Chris Gibbons, who had established himself on both Radio 702 and Cape Talk, to Jerusalem and Ramallah, with the idea that Chris spend time here, continue doing his South African shows from here and introduce a similar show that focused on economic issues. Chris liked the idea and Issie thought it may be a creative way to bring in commercial traffic.

We also began in earnest to explore the idea of selling our news bulletins to radio stations around the globe, to bring in much needed revenues.

Whilst all of this was happening, the Israelis appointed a new Minister of Communications, the leader of the religious and right wing Shas party, Eli Yashi. I made Issie aware on one of his many visits that we ought to be concerned, but he did not take it seriously and simply dismissed it out of hand, thinking all his bases were covered—much to our peril, as we later learned.

All in all, Issie was literally carrying the radio station financially and facing lots of pressure, especially from those around him. Once he even lost his cool and angrily retorted that he was not a philanthropist.

Anyway, the warning bells began ringing, when his son, William got himself a guru, Rabbi Yossi, from the Shas party, even marrying a woman the good rabbi chose for him, though she was divorced and came along with children. William was considered to be one of the most eligible bachelors in South Africa and he had the pick of the field. Issie was disappointed but learned to live with it. William and his rabbi were keen on getting Issie to set-up a religious radio station instead of RAM FM.

Another duty, I willingly bore was that of minute taker at all board meetings. We had them mostly in Tel Aviv, save for a couple in Jerusalem. Board members attended and Issie who chaired them consulted and moved along with his vision. Anyway, it was mostly his money.

It was during a meeting in Tel Aviv in February 2008, Issie's brother Natie, a billionaire based in the USA, joined us, as he had contributed a generous sum of money to move the station forward. We were presented with an amazing marketing campaign by Guy Bar, creative director of Gitam BBDO, the agency that created it. "The station views music as being a universal language that can cross all borders and reach all people, all nations and all religions" was the basis of the campaign.

We were floored with the presentation and the campaign was to be launched at the airport with passports of various countries that bore pictures of star musicians and bands, made up ingeniously with collages of visa entry stamps, handed to persons and then at various spots in Tel Aviv. Later the ads would be placed on billboards on the Ayalon freeway and other localities and then on buses in Jerusalem. On the Palestinian side, billboards would be placed on the major road linking Ramallah to Jerusalem—unusual for an ad campaign with the same images used in both places.

The advertising campaign featured The Beatles, Bob Marley, Elton John, and many others. The one that featured the Beatles had a picture perfect image of the fab-four made up from visa stamps and the slogan that caught one's eye read: "Even though they have not visited every country, their music has" and below in bold followed, Music Has No Boundaries. 93.6 RAM FM. In a box on the side it read, "Broadcast from Jerusalem and Ramallah" below which our website and additional frequency was noted www.ramfm.net Also 87.7 FM

The huge billboards on the Ayalon freeway linking Tel Aviv with Jerusalem and Haifa made a stunning impact, as well as the others in Israel, and then buses in Jerusalem were running all over the holy city with the ads. On the Palestinian side, the road leading to and from Jerusalem had smaller ones placed on the lamp poles. You couldn't miss it.

Gitam launched it with a huge media campaign and we were all over the news.

For the campaign, Gitam won a prestigious American advertising award related to the design, which spoke volumes about an expensive campaign to increase awareness and listenership, something we kept learning about with scores of new callers, whom we could identify, thanks to technology, we had a system that logged in all the details of callers and it gave us a fair indication of frequency of calls and callers as well as where they were based on both sides of the divide.

Thanks to the campaign, RAM FM was everywhere, in the spotlight and in your face, which then made some people realize that we were in fact, making a difference and we had to be stopped.

6 Closure of RAM FM
Staying alive until the bitter end

IT WAS MONDAY AFTERNOON, 6 APRIL 2008: Maysoun and I were in northern Tel Aviv, meeting with the CEO of Dealbox to conclude a sponsorship deal for an economic program.

The phone rang, it was May on the line. "Maysoun," she said, "the police are here. They pulled the plug, we are switched off, they are removing all the equipment, they are closing us down!

"Take it easy May, we are coming back to Jerusalem now," Maysoun responded. Maysoun was shocked as I was with this unexpected development, especially that RAM FM had established a huge listenership and commercial traffic was finally on its way. The future was looking bright. And we had just concluded a deal with Emirates Airways prior to this sponsorship with Dealbox.

Without any hesitation, we had to end our meeting, and then drive back in haste to Jerusalem to find out what was the case.

I drove while Maysoun postulated on what may be the reason for the police to suddenly come along and shut us down. We were legal, could it be political?

We couldn't place our finger on it, although I said in jest, "While Israel is building walls, we are finding the ties that bind and building bridges, and that may be the reason."

Arriving at the Technology Gardens Park building in Malcha, where our Jerusalem studios were housed, and on our way up to the escalators, we met an employee of Contact Productions, the Israeli company that hosted us, as they did Al Jazeera television and many other international media. Arik, with concern marked all over his face, advised, "The police are arresting everyone, run away!"

I looked at Maysoun and said, "We have done no wrong, and if a ship goes down, the captain goes down with it." Without hesitation, Maysoun headed up the escalator and I tagged along.

Entering the offices of RAM FM, we were greeted by a sea of bewildered staff, police in uniform and some in plain clothes, busy ripping off all the studio equipment, computers from the offices and any other radio related paraphernalia and packing them in boxes for removal.

One policeman was seated and busy taking down all the details of the station's personnel.

I instructed Maysoun, "Please don't say a word, until we know what we have done and what the charges are, if any." All our colleagues seemed dumbfounded and I sensed fear as we made fleeting eye-contact.

Maysoun was very agitated, and I tried to calm her down, "These guys are only following orders, let's cooperate with them and soon this misunderstanding shall sort itself out."

Once all the equipment was hauled and loaded into a police truck, we were escorted out of the offices, but not before some international television stations, housed in the building, learned of the police presence and rushed over to capture the arrest, closure, and loading of the equipment.

We were then seated in several police vehicles and driven to the Talpiot Police Station.

It was my first-ever ride in a police car. No one was talking. And as we weaved through the Jerusalem afternoon traffic, I wondered if this was the end of 93.6 RAM FM.

Early evening, we arrived at the Talpiot police station, we disembarked from the police cars and were then led down a corridor, into the lower levels of the building—beginning of being sealed off from the outside world—into a dark and dingy room, where a young officer was tasked to write down charge sheets for each one.

I learned from him we were going to be questioned individually. Still no idea what was our crime and what we were being charged for.

My mind was racing. We lived in an apartment in Ramallah with our son Adam, who had a nanny taking care of him, but at the end of each day, she headed back to Bethlehem to be with her own family. We were way below ground level of the police station and there was no mobile phone signal. What was I going to do? How long are we going to be there? And what if the worst was to become of us? What about Adam, who looked forward to seeing mummy and daddy at the end of each day?

I noticed Maysoun's teary eyes, she too was concerned about Adam.

While all these questions were occupying my thoughts, I became somewhat perturbed when a few Palestinian colleagues were not being cooperative with the police officer, and in defiance resorted to singing their freedom songs. I interjected, "This guy is simply doing his job. He did not arrest us. He does not even know why we are here. Please let's cooperate with him and get this over and done with so that we can then all go home."

The young Israeli police officer looked at me, approvingly and smiled.

After which everyone cooperated with him to get their respective charge sheets completed.

Finally, it was my turn, "What do you do at the station?"

"I am the driver" and in a sense, I really was.

He then beckoned to me to leave and leave I did as quickly as I could, but not before I looked at Maysoun and indicated she needn't be concerned about Adam.

As soon as I got out of the police station building into the breezy Jerusalem evening, I noticed that it was dark, and the streets were empty. Luckily for me, I was able to hail a passing cab to take me to the American Colony hotel in East Jerusalem, from whence I got a Palestinian cab to Kalandia Checkpoint, crossed it, and then took another cab to our home in Ramallah.

I was, most certainly, not going back to the parking lot at the Jerusalem studio, where our car was, for fear that I may be re-arrested there.

Arriving home, I was greeted by a worried looking nanny and a pleased Adam, who leaped into my arms.

Later I learned from Maysoun that when the arresting officers came to collect all the RAM FM personnel for individual questioning, they were visibly upset that the young officer let me get away. According to them, I was the one they really wanted to talk to.

From the comfort of my home, I then called Issie whom I got hold of on his mobile phone. He was, at the time, visiting family in Denver, Colorado. After I calmly broke the news to him, he called Cookie, his trusted lawyer, who immediately got onto the case.

After putting Adam to bed, who seemed to be agitated that mummy was not home, I was then literally on the phone for the entire night, liaising with Cookie, who traveled to Jerusalem. I learned that we were charged for operating a radio station without a license. Cookie knew our set-up, but I once more explained to him that our radio license was issued by the Palestinians and we were totally legal, assuring him that in the morning I would obtain a copy of the license and forward it to him. He indicated that he was powerless to obtain the release of anyone, and we had to simply wait for the morning, when all would be arraigned in Court.

Thereafter, I made phone calls to all parents and spouses of those spending the night in prison. I learned from Cookie that they were taken to the Russian Compound, a place with a reputation that preceded it. Later, I also learned that all the guys were placed in a communal cell with common criminals and the women, including Maysoun, were placed in a similar cell with one woman who was on a murder charge. Like most cells, they were filthy and the humiliation of spending the night with common criminals, and not even knowing the charges, was traumatic for all of them.

And then international media picked up the story, and my phone continuously rang into the early hours of the morning. All the while, I was confused as to why our equipment was ripped off and why all the personnel were arrested. We were NOT a pirate station, our license was issued by the Palestinians, we were broadcasting from Ramallah, and a microwave link hooked up our studios in Ramallah and Jerusalem, and whatever we produced in Jerusalem was sent back to Ramallah to be broadcast from there. It was all legitimate, so I smelled a political reason for the closure.

I then called Mark Regev, the spokesperson for prime minister Ehud Olmert. Mark had visited our Jerusalem studios and even hosted me for lunch and a discussion at the Malcha mall. He knew we were a legitimate radio station. After listening to our predicament, he said: "This is Israel. Here the angels have more power than god. My prime minister cannot help, as he too is in trouble with the angels." That spoke volumes.

Another person of influence was far more philosophical when I approached him. He said, "In Israel, every day has it's dog and today that the dog is RAM FM"

In the morning, as soon as our nanny arrived, I headed to the studio in Ramallah, with added responsibilities to keep the station on air minus Jerusalem and its personnel.

Luckily, Martin B had left after his breakfast show and he was not taken away, as his producer Francis unfortunately was. We asked our faithful driver, Dawood, to bring in Martin to do the breakfast show from Ramallah and provided him a local producer, and the show went on, regardless.

We opted not to talk about what had happened to us, and continue with business as usual, although all our listeners and fans wished to know. My standard response was, "Until the Israeli authorities decide what crime we have committed; we shall reserve our right to comment."

After Martin's show, I continued with my show, but since both Mike and Arda were holed in prison, I sat-in for their show—six hours on air after no sleep, but thanks to coffee, coffee, and a determination to keep the station alive, I managed. Kevin continued with the drive show and all seemed well with RAM FM, on the surface, at least.

At lunch, we learned that the personnel were escorted out of their cells, after being strapped around their ankles in chains, and taken to the court. Cookie had cut a deal with the prosecution, who brought an additional charge, after we had proven our legality, and the new charge was that we were affecting the airport frequencies and thus endangering the security of the state of Israel—serious indeed!

True to form, whenever all else fails Israel trumps up security.

So, the best Cookie could get was bail and house arrest for all, for fifteen days, with each person compelled to wear a band, for the police to monitor their movements, and they were also banned from communicating with anyone—almost like solitary confinement. Although everyone thought this was unjust and humiliating to say the least, Cookie assured me and Issie, who was in constant phone contact with both of us, that under the circumstances, it was the only deal he could have obtained.

Maysoun had to remain in Jerusalem, cut-off from Adam, but I assured her that no matter what, I would bring Adam to her every evening, even though it was in violation of the deal Cookie obtained.

That afternoon, I arranged a meeting with parents and spouses of those under house arrest in Jerusalem and explained the case to them, assuring them that Issie and Cookie were taking care of things and Issie was emphatic, he would take care of his people. To my utter surprise and disgust, some of them now sought financial compensation for the suffering their loved ones had undergone. Now that was something!

Then one spouse suddenly became the reporter for South African media on the case, and she wanted to know everything, whilst we were playing our cards close to our chests as the investigation was continuing and no formal charges were yet laid.

When the police alleged that we were a pirate station, we showed them our license, and when they claimed that we were affecting the airport, we brought in technical experts, who proved beyond any doubt, with readings that our transmitters were fitted with proper filters and thus not doing as alleged.

Anyway, Mark's wife, Peroshnee who was reporting for South African media, concocted a story, that I was not transparent with them and complained directly to Issie. To defuse the situation and to placate her, Issie instructed Xolani to then take care of the families. Anyway, Cookie and I were busy dealing with the case and Xolani got his brief from me, but it did relieve me of a burden I was not keen to bear.

That very afternoon, I was interviewed on Israeli radio, to explain our side of the story and I used the occasion to even advertise our station, which I mused, was kind of cute. Following that interview, I went live on Israeli television, in whose studios I even met the spokesman for the Israeli ministry of foreign affairs, whom I had interviewed on many occasions and he too expressed surprise at the sudden turn of events.

My explanation on television was, "Pirates hide, we are out in the open, as we are a legitimate radio station with a license from the Palestinian side. Jerusalem was simply manufacturing products and sending it back via a microwave link to Ramallah from whence it was being broadcast. And the fact that we exposed ourselves with such a huge advertising campaign meant clearly, we were not a pirate radio station. On the issue of the charge related to Israeli security and the airport, I asked the question, why after almost two years? And anyway, our technical experts prepared a report and submitted it to the authorities that the allegation about us affecting the airport was totally unfounded."

Then it was a long drive to go back to Ramallah, and a return visit with Adam to his mummy and finally back home, exhausted with a sleeping child. And the rest of the night my phone kept ringing, as local, regional and international media were continually pursuing the story.

I was managing the station in Maysoun's absence, doing two shows for six hours a day, talking to the media and playing mummy to Adam—it sure called on all my reserves, in staying alive.

After the fifteen-day period elapsed, the wrist bands were removed from the imprisoned staff and their restrictions were lifted. They were free to return to work.

By this time, we had hired a car for Martin to drive every morning to Ramallah for his show and Arda came to Ramallah and did her show from there, hooking up with Mike on the phone, who traveled daily from his home in Tel Aviv and sat in the studio-less offices in Jerusalem. The news team mostly moved to Ramallah, but some provided news feeds from Jerusalem.

All in all, RAM FM, having lost Jerusalem, continued on-air from Ramallah and without missing too many beats.

Issie, kind as always, instructed Maysoun to take the entire team and their spouses or partners for a week-end holiday, at his personal expense, to the holiday resort of Eilat on the Red Sea, which we all did. And a most wonderful time was had by all, save for two Palestinians who could not obtain Israeli permits to leave the West Bank.

While the legal issues were being handled by Cookie and his office, we obtained indications that should Issie arrive in Israel, he would be arrested. But that was not the case, and Issie made the trip anyway. Maysoun and I met him for dinner at his favorite hotel in Jerusalem, The King David, where he immediately informed us, "I was taken by Rabbi Yossi to meet with Rabbi Obeda Josef; he blessed my project and me. He gave me a Bharuch (Jewish blessing)."

I did not buy this, as the religious head of the ultra-right Shas Party, which was responsible for our closure in the first place, known for his rabid and anti-Palestinian views, even referring to them as cockroaches could ever have done so. That is when I knew Issie was not being wholly truthful and somehow, I knew on that fateful dinner that the writing was on the wall. Issie had made up his mind or it was being done for him, to close down the station.

As we left, Maysoun tried not to accept my reading, somehow convincing herself that the station was still going to continue. We drove back home, in deadly silence, save for the music of RAM FM.

On a lighter note, I hosted, once a month, a most popular Israeli psychic, Rikki Kitaro, who was, in a word, amazing! Her presence on my talk show lit up all the phone lines and it was entertaining and fun, as she told listeners all about their lives. Her accuracy was uncanny!

Kevin and I decided on a Friday to drive to her seaside home in Caesarea in the north of Israel and meet her face to face to obtain personal readings. Cutting to the chase, one of the many predictions she made was, "Your radio station is going to be closed down." Which at the time, I did not take seriously. Now it seemed that she was on the crystal ball.

And then that moment came, on a cold and snowy Ramallah winter's morning, Maysoun and I were summoned by Issie to Tel Aviv to a meeting at the Hilton Hotel. We got there with a snow-covered car, amidst much consternation, at the very hotel where the idea of the radio station began in the year 2003.

Issie convened the meeting and then took the decision to pull the plug on RAM FM, but took great pains to put a spin to the closure. He had the Israeli PR company, Gitam Porto Novelli personnel with him. They drafted a statement that I was instructed to read on air, after the news, the next morning, and then literally pull the plug later in the day.

The decision was made and there was nothing Maysoun and I could do to change it.

We shook hands and I reminded Issie of our first meeting in that very hotel and how uncannily it all had to end there. Life does circle one's dreams and aspirations.

It was certainly sad, but we had to focus on another task on hand—to pull the plug, close shop and find new careers and begin lives anew.

Maysoun and I left soon afterwards and as we drove to Ramallah we reminisced on the great journey and wonderful experiences we had with RAM FM, and like all good things it had to end. Her job was to undo all we had done, indeed a mammoth task.

The next day, after the midday news bulletin, I walked into the studio, read out from the prepared script, with tears streaming down my face, "I am here to inform you that RAM FM will discontinue its broadcast this evening at 7 pm. Although we are aware that RAM FM had successfully achieved its vision to establish a platform for dialogue and understanding, this decision was taken by the board of directors following an inability of the station to generate sufficient advertising revenues to sustain its ongoing operations. We thank you for being with us during the time we were on-air. I'm Raf Gangat saying . . . Goodbye!"

Followed with the station jingle, "Music has no boundaries, 93.6 RAM FM." And then, we played, for the last time, our wonderful selection of music.

At 7 pm I came back on-air to say, "We began our test broadcast in February 2006, followed by our official launch in February 2007. Thanks for being loyal listeners, we certainly had a wonderful time together. On behalf of the RAM FM family, I'm Raf Gangat bidding you goodbye and God bless!"

And then like we began, we brought the curtain down with The Beatles song, "Give Peace a Chance."

Always philosophical, I reflected that my ship was once again sailing on uncharted territory, forever blown by the winds of change, the story of my life!

When the song ended, I pulled the plug on 93.6 RAM FM, the English radio station that crossed boundaries, created a bridge over troubled waters and brought so many people closer, but like most noble initiatives in the Holy land of conflict, it too met a premature end.

The spin was financial consideration, especially the lack of advertising revenues, led to the closure of the station, which in a sense was true. But I knew it was not the whole truth.

Now let me cite the real reason or reasons for the closure. Pressure was building on Issie, directed by Tami and her partners at Radio Tel Aviv, who saw us as a serious competitor, as our signal was excellent in Tel Aviv and our music was far superior to anything they could dish out. They convinced Issie that the renewal of their Tel Aviv license, wherein Issie was also a shareholder, was in jeopardy if Issie continued to have RAM FM on air and it was in all their interests to close it down. Truth be told, it was a lie! We were a competitor and it was a ploy to get us out of the way—as Issie learned later, much to his anger, when they even worked him out of his shares at Radio Tel Aviv.

Maysoun and I later met Anat, the CEO of Sharpa, the agency that handles advertising for all radio stations in Israel. Anat assured us that we were very popular and if we focused on music and cut-out the politics, she could easily fill all our advertising slots. In fact, she even walked us to her own car and made us note what she was listening to on her radio—her dial was set on 93.6 RAM FM. She told us, "You are a serious competitor to Israeli radio stations, and you have taken away many listeners from Radio Tel Aviv."

Then there was the issue of undue pressure on Issie from his son and his rabbi, to divest the equipment from RAM FM in Palestine in order to set-up a religious radio station, as they convinced him that he was wasting his time with his peace project and a religious one would be much more fruitful.

We also learned that an Israeli radio station with Russian mafia backing had set us up. Let me explain this. Our technical consultant, Sergey, the Russian from whom we purchased our transmitters and who provided ongoing technical services to enhance our signal, especially in Jerusalem where the terrain was always working against us, played us and most probably was handsomely rewarded for doing so.

We had two transmitters and two frequencies broadcasting from Ramallah, but we later learned that Sergey had set-up a repeater on the roof of the Holiday Inn Crowne Plaza, where he was hosting an Israeli radio station. He pointed this out to his contacts in the Israeli Communications Ministry, literally giving them reason to declare it an illegal broadcast instrument and thus provide them the pretext for our closure.

Once Jerusalem was closed, Sergey conveniently made a disappearing act.

After having spent much time figuring out the circumstances that led to the closure in Jerusalem—let me provide another very plausible reason—what started the ball rolling against us was our advertising campaign. I have always maintained that attention to detail is key when one is changing the rules as we did, and this is where we certainly slipped up.

I learned from a journalist with the Jerusalem Post that bus shelters that carried our posters were defaced in the religious neighborhoods and rabbis were not impressed with our campaign ads singing out from the buses and that many, many Haredi kids were listening to RAM FM.

The rabbis pointed this out to Shas, the religious party in whose hands the ministry of communication resided, for them to stop this station and the minister instructed his people to do accordingly. Our mistake was that our campaign stated "Broadcast from Jerusalem & Ramallah" which was not true, as we had studios in both cities but broadcast only from Ramallah and a microwave link did the necessary as I explained earlier.

The police then removed the equipment and arrested our people for operating an illegal radio station in Jerusalem. When we produced authentic papers to prove that we were legal, the airport and air traffic disruption was cited as a security issue, but after we technically showed that it was not the case, Sergey stepped in as concurrently the issue of competition came into play and he served the needs of his paymasters by providing them the so-called rod or repeater or smoking gun which then made us illegal.

All in all, it was a technical slip-up in our huge advertising campaign that created enemies. It was our competitors, it was Sergey working against us and most importantly it was both religious and political, as the right in Israel wanted us out. To them, Palestine and its people are non-people who do not exist, and peaceful co-existence is not in their cards. So, the spin that it was a financial consideration was not wholly true.

Anyway, always with a never-say-die attitude, though we had lost the battle, I was ready to fight on to win this war—a war for peace!

I called Issie and asked him if he was prepared to sell the station's equipment. He agreed to do so, as it would save him all the hassles of removing and transporting it to Israel and storing it and then probably selling it later. We agreed on staggered terms of payment.

This was all we needed and Maysoun and I then scheduled a meeting with senior American diplomats involved in media, and their colleagues in Jerusalem at the American consulate. It was at that meeting, we learned how popular we were and the difference we were making.

I then began to draft a comprehensive proposal for funds to pay for the equipment, to keep the station going and pay salaries for basic staff. The Americans proposed to even bring in professional consultants to help us become commercially sustainable. In short, we were offered a one-year lifeline and that was all we needed. However, the Americans insisted that we should increase the talk content and I should do it, as most of them keenly listened to my show "Talk @10."

This was not what Sharpa wanted but our financers had the right to dictate otherwise, and we were not complaining. All that mattered to us was that we would be back on air.

Maysoun and I agreed to re-launch with a skeleton staff: she as the station manager, myself as the morning/talk show host, Kevin as the music manager/afternoon show host, Mark as the news head, assisted by two reporters and a basic administration component—a lean and mean team to journey us via the bridge over troubled waters that the Americans had so kindly offered to lay on for us.

Concurrently, Mark Otte, the European ambassador responsible for the Middle East peace process, and whom I had interviewed on a couple of occasions in our Ramallah studios, offered another lifeline. He was approached by European diplomats stationed in Ramallah, who had also visited the Palestinian Ministry of Telecommunications. We were informed by the deputy minister that all wanted to assist us in whatever way or means at their disposal for us to stay on air and it was nice to know this.

Working fervently, I completed the proposal with a detailed business plan and submitted it to the Americans. As it was going through the normal bureaucratic process; I was seized on doing something similar for Mark Otte and the Europeans.

Let me now explain what we did in the interim with the transmitter and signal.

Initially we pulled the plug as Issie instructed and shut down, but after we got a sense of hope from the Americans and Issie's willingness to sell the station's equipment to us, we switched it on to hold-on to the 93.6 and 87.7 frequencies which we had paid for and legally owned, but we played NO music, just a beep transmission sound covered these two frequencies.

However, when we obtained the green light from the Americans, Kevin, fired-up in excitement, began to once more play our RAM FM brand of music, which suddenly got all our listeners very excited. He was on email contact with scores of them. They were like junkies missing their daily musical fix— guess RAM FM was addictive.

It was still a matter of days before the USAID approval and funds were scheduled to be granted.

And then on a Friday morning, as I was driving to Jerusalem, I received a call from Issie, who was irate to say the least, after he had learned from his people at Radio Tel Aviv that we were back on air. He instructed me to immediately switch off the music we were playing and if we did not the Israeli army would be coming that night to smash up the equipment.

This threat was apparently conveyed to him by Rabbi Yossi, who had indicated that his contacts in the Shas-controlled ministry of communications had advised him so. Furthermore, Issie informed me, according to Tami from Radio Tel Aviv, we were jeopardizing the renewal of their license.

My hands were tied, Issie was still the boss and it was his prerogative to call the shots, as the USAID lifeline hadn't been thrown yet. I assured him that we would switch off immediately and called Kevin to do the necessary, which he reluctantly did.

As a South African project, we had radio experience as well as institutional knowledge in reconciliation and nation building, which we had hoped to bring to this region. I pondered on this missed opportunity as I drove back to Ramallah.

On my return to Ramallah, I scheduled an urgent meeting with the deputy minister of telecommunications and sought his assistance, telling him that the Palestinians provided us the license which we paid for and they ought to protect us against the Israelis, and he responded "We cannot even protect the president, the Israelis can come in at any time and take him out, that is our reality."

So, we had no option, but to accept Rabbi Yossi's warning and let it be.

It all made sense then. We were protected with Issie's (a South African Jew's) connections in Israel, but once he opted to leave us, we were vulnerable, and we had no option but to throw in the towel, though we stood up after having been knocked down before and fought on awhile.

That was it, the fight was over, the war was lost. In the end, it was a political decision to unplug RAM FM.

The next week, the Americans informed us that our proposal was approved, but it was a few days too late.

Issie's lawyer Cookie then made all the necessary arrangements to sell the station's equipment for a song, with all the office equipment included, to Tariq Abbas, the son of the Palestinian president, who transformed it into an Arabic-only music station. He obtained a toy at a bargain-basement price, something he had always desired, and Issie had rid himself of the headache but then he ended up being conned out of Radio Tel Aviv, by Tami and her partners.

Issie's last words were, "I want nothing to do with Israel."

Issie paid all, according to the dictates of the Palestinian labor laws, but Maysoun and I had no legal contracts with him, it was only a verbal agreement. For having been taken down the road to damnation by Cookie, Tami, and her partners, he seemingly lashed out at those closest to him and that was us, paying off Maysoun and me, a pittance compared to what was really due.

I was unplugged! And to compound matters, my Israeli visa expired, and the Israeli Interior Ministry wanted me out.

Martin B, our breakfast show host, immediately found himself a job with a Jordanian based English radio station and moved across the river to Amman. Kevin Lee, the drive show host and music manager, remained with the new owner of the equipment Tariq Abbas, but moved to Tel Aviv into the IT sector later. Mike Brand, co-host of the afternoon show, found himself a position with an Israeli radio station and Arda, his partner, moved into the Palestinian NGO sector. And as for our news team, Tyson went on to become a fully-fledged rabbi. Shireen moved to Press TV and then later to Radio Sawwa in the USA. Xolani went back to Johannesburg and landed on Radio 702. Mark returned home and Ashira had a stint with BBC and then came back to work in the Palestinian NGO sector. Abdullah moved to the presidency in Ramallah taking care of foreign journalists and our administration staff. All got paid out their severance and moved on, but the memories linger. . .

RAM FM left a mark on its faithful band of listeners. Some said, we were simply ahead of our time, others said, we were doomed right from the very beginning, I said, "At least we gave peace a chance."

7 Post-Ram FM

Re-inventing myself, starting a new.

L IFE TENDS TO PLAY GAMES: just when you think you are going places, you return full-circle, to where you began. With the closure of RAM FM, I headed back to Weenen in South Africa, where my circle began, but not after having forwarded my CV with sound clips of my talk and music shows to numerous radio stations with no success whatsoever.

In Weenen, I was back with my aging parents and relaxing in the tranquility of my hometown. With regular forays across the road to the river for some angling or simply to while away the time, I contemplated the beginning of a new road, all the while indulging in my mum's incredible culinary delights—indeed a most welcome relief from whence I had come from.

What am I going to do with my life now? What do I have to offer? Years of knowledge and experience in communication, media and diplomacy is what I am!

One morning, while my mum was busy cleaning her attic, I opted to lend a hand. I discovered boxes of books I had left behind from way back. Upon opening them, I found files and notes from courses I attended at the Leadership Institute of South Africa, as well as lots of interesting and relevant material from my diplomatic training days. Scanning through them, I couldn't help but marvel at my journey since those heady days and how I had come back home.

I pondered on how useful most of that material would be for Palestine, which was at the stage that South Africa once was, when I first got sight of the material. From that moment onwards, a new path was somehow destined for me. In a sense, discovering it was godsend!

After charging my batteries in Weenen, I headed to Pretoria and Johannesburg to meet with my friends, to explore the possibilities of getting into business, maybe give free reign to my entrepreneurial spirit. Sadly, I learned from this encounter, it was all about whom you knew and how you could either bribe or bring the person into the deal, which was the game in vogue. Being the person I am, there was no way in which I could align myself with these corrupt business modus operandi.

The problem with capitalism is that it best rewards the worst part in us: ruthless, competitive, conniving, opportunistic, acquisitive drives, giving

Life after RAM FM

little reward and often much punishment, or at least much handicap, to honesty, compassion, fair play, many forms of arduous work, love of justice, and a concern for those in need.

So, I headed once more to the Holy Land of conflict where my heart and soul lay—it was beckoning me to return.

I landed in Tel Aviv, armed with all my discovered material, but firstly there was the pressing matter of renewing my visa.

When I first got to the Holy Land, I was a diplomat and passing through the airport was a breeze, thereafter as a journalist issued with a press card from the Israeli government was easy too, but now I was simply an ordinary person married to an Arab/Palestinian and I accordingly was given the same treatment that my wife and her people were subject to daily and this became a new experience. Being stripped naked and humiliated by kids brandishing weapons was not easy to handle.

At the Israeli ministry of interior, I encountered a rude and obnoxious woman who initially refused to extend my visa. I told her, "I am married to a citizen of Jerusalem and I have a son, and you want me to go back? What about my family?" Her retort, "Take them with you!"

My blood was boiling, as I was dealing with a Russian Jew who had come to Israel because of her race, whilst I could not be there with my wife and son who were both born there. Another kind of apartheid, I thought.

Nevertheless, I realized that this was one fight I was not going to win, as the dice was loaded against me. In the end and after much pleading, she reluctantly gave me a month, to sort my matters and leave, but not before making me sign a letter that I would in fact do so.

I was screwed!

Meanwhile Maysoun had landed a job with a USAID contractor working on enhancing the ' rule of law' in Palestine. She was the communications and media officer for an organization headed by a corrupt and idiotic Palestinian who had no legal background whatsoever, but had employed many legal experts to do the work for him. Apparently, he was 'connected' and abused his position without any limits. She was frustrated by the whole set-up and often cried, but she needed the job, at least to pay the rent, as our meager savings were fast dwindling.

Times were difficult, but at least we had a roof over our heads and food on the table and for that we were thankful.

Not long thereafter, I bumped into my friend Jane Masri, an American married to one of the richest Palestinians. She owned an advertising company and she was a huge fan of RAM FM. After indicating how much she missed listening to us, she then inquired, "So Raf, what are you doing these days?"

"I am looking for a job."

"A USAID contractor is looking for a communications and media consultant, are you interested?"

I was more than interested and I immediately fired off my CV to her. The next day, I was called in by the contractor, Chemonics. Their project was designed to enhance various Palestinian ministries. My task was to do an evaluation of the ministry of transport's communication and media and thereafter set in motion, a plan of action to improve it, including a complete action plan for a road safety campaign. Furthermore, I was to evaluate the government spokesperson bureau and offer recommendations.

It was my first ever consultancy business after RAM FM and it was like going back to work, in an office environment and I felt kind of strange. However, the best thing that could have ever happened and for which I am forever grateful was that the Americans organized to have my visa extended by a year.

Going to work at an eight to four job, sitting in an open-plan office and becoming like everyone else was something I had to adapt to quickly. Working within an aid organization, was where I gained valuable experience, and it propelled me onto a new career.

This is what Chris, the head of Chemonics, had to say about my completed work, in an email dated, 8 May 2009, "I reviewed the two assessments you provided me in hard copy. They are both excellent. They are short, clear, concise—with actionable recommendations that are in line with our project objectives. I look forward to sending these on to USAID."

Chris was the most forthright with me, "We do not make money out of you. You are not Palestinian or American and our profits are calculated on a multiplier effect, based on what we pay you. So, I am sorry, we cannot use your services in future."

After this stint, I landed straight into the Palestinian Non-Governmental Sector (PNGO), to do an assignment for PNGO, the umbrella body for all the Palestinian NGOs.

From a consultant, I became a media trainer, working with a group of media persons from various NGOs and training them on communicating messages through radio and television. Besides the lectures, we did numerous radio and television interviews, debates, talk shows etc. using the studios of a local television station. Theory internalized through actual work, was indeed gratifying for me to facilitate.

But I still yearned for radio.

Thereafter, I received a call from a Palestinian Academic Dr Ghassan Khatib, who informed me that he was appointed by the prime minister as the government spokesperson, exactly as I had recommended to Chemonics and USAID.

I felt a sense of achievement and excitement, having noted that with South Africa, the liberation movements were so engaged in the so-called struggle that no one prepared for the morning after, a price we paid and continue paying for, for not having done so.

Palestine, on the other hand, with prime minister Salaam Fayyad, was steaming ahead with building all the institutions of state, for the morning after. However, the liberation aspect was being neglected. Somehow a healthy balance ought to be obtained, but that was the business of Palestinians, although a friend once said in jest, "Raf is a Palestinian wannabe."

For the next three months, I worked with Ghassan on restructuring the government press office and proposed that he heads all the spokespersons from the various ministries. I designed a communications and media training course for all the spokespersons, to be facilitated by me at the Center for Continuing Education (CCE) which is linked to Birzeit University and I insisted that as a bonus for successful completion, each participant should not only receive a certificate, but a salary increase as well. This whole exercise took a great deal of time and effort, and I felt that it would be most useful, having noted that, "Palestine is a remarkable story, but the storytellers are wanting." In the end, for all my work, I was not even paid a single bean. Ghassan informed me that the Palestinian cabinet did not have funds to proceed.

Later I learned that my work was handed to a British organization (DIFRD) who not only funded it but brought in their own experts to facilitate it and the university made money for hosting it, but then the participants learned absolutely nothing. One participant even informed me that British consultants, who were paid handsomely, recited histories and academic superfluous stuff, whereas what they sought were tools and skills, which was my modus operandi.

Meanwhile, back in South Africa, Mo Shaik was appointed head of State Security Agency (SSA) and since he was a colleague and friend from my time in Foreign Affairs, I sent him a congratulatory note and wished him well in his new job. He immediately came back to me that he was interested in using my knowledge and experience of the region, which I thought was flattering. And it followed with a communication, "Hold tight, one of my guys will see you soon."

A few months later, I was instructed by the Ramallah based SSA guy to meet with him and his boss at a local coffee shop, where I was surprised to see that Padime, whom I knew from my time as a diplomat in Ramallah and whom I considered a non-bright spark, now headed the Middle East Division in SSA. I kept my judgment in check and listened to what he had to say. Padime was interested in setting up an NGO in a place which suffers from a glut of them and then to use it as an intelligence gathering front, an outdated and useless idea.

I explained why his idea was a non-starter and suggested an alternative. The Middle East Region is the biggest media story in the world, and receives in proportion more attention than any other region. The world's media is based here, reporting on the conflict as it unfolds, and my personal experience over the years, firstly as a diplomat and then as a media person, has taught me that being a professional media person provides one with access to just about everyone and more so, access to information. Stories for public consumption are generally based on spin, but the real story lies in relationships and the individual touch. This I developed through my stint with RAM FM, as the morning talk show host and general gofer for the station.

My suggestion: I be appointed the SABC correspondent for the Middle East. This is NOT a Palestinian/Israeli conflict, but a Middle East conflict with the involvement of regional players that impact on the primary conflict. My role would be to provide, on the ground, stories behind the stories with the emphasis on interviews with key role players, as the general footage is readily available and easily obtainable by the SABC from the various media agencies based here. My radio and television expertise would hold me in good stead, but a visit to the SABC in Auckland Park and a meeting with the principals to agree on the modus operandi would be crucial to get this off the ground. Local and regional camera crews are available for hire at short notice, with professional production studios for satellite transmission to SABC. As for radio, a home office setup with a computer, phone, mic and processor could be easily rigged and stories may be recorded and emailed whenever required.

All in all, the SABC would be provided with reporting, both for radio and television, by a South African who began his career with SABC radio and through a diplomatic career, has acquainted himself extremely well with the issues in the Middle East Region, and has built a network of media contacts. Within this context I shall, with access to persons and information, be able to provide quality intelligence and analysis, not only on the Israeli/Palestinian conflict, but moving into the region with issues related to Lebanon, Syria, Iraq, Iran, Egypt, Saudi Arabia and Yemen. All of this would be obtained through interaction with media persons and travels to meet and to interview various role players. The possibilities media opens up are endless, it provides a valuable resource that cannot be emphasized enough.

We parted, and I heard no more. Mo resigned and Padime came back to Ramallah on a second posting to head the SSA office—enough said!

In between all of this, I approached Dr Sari Nusseibeh, the head of Al Quds university in Jerusalem about a possible lecturing job, as I was still unemployed. Since I knew him from my diplomatic days, he was most excited, and he passed on my details to his deputy and it wasn't long before I was requested to meet with Sari's wife, Lucy, who headed the media division of the university.

I indicated that without a license, I could set-up a university Internet radio station. Al Quds University had an educational television station, stationed at the Institute of Modern Media (IMM) in Ramallah, which had its limitations by being terrestrial in an environment that had progressed rapidly to satellite transmissions, which flooded viewing options for the public, including the students.

Since 90% of Palestinians had access to computers with relatively cheap high speed service, the potential it offered as an alternative to the limitations imposed by the saturation of radio frequencies, weak signals and ongoing issues with the Israelis was significant. I advised that the university set up an Internet radio station at the Institute of Modern Media. Also, the Internet offered so much more in terms of new media; like Facebook and Twitter and the connectivity with cellular phones, and it even offered an enhancement to Al Quds Television with live-linkages.

Internet Radio at IMM, which we intended to name, RADIO 1, would provide information and entertainment but most importantly serve an educational purpose. The home page would be linked to Google, Facebook and Twitter and various university educational sites.

About the content—the intent was to begin with music, both English and Arabic and then obtain feedback from students via the Internet on what they desired and build the content and programming according to their needs, and I was to lead on this journey.

The technical set-up would cost in the region of about $3,000 to $5,000 and the entire set-up could be completed in a short space of time. Thereafter I would require funds to cover my cost as the consultant, to train students in various aspects of radio, arrange the content and programming and monitor the development of the radio station as it evolved, for at least six months.

Academic freedom demands free speech and although it is the democratic right of Palestinian youth in general, this is not the case. Several reasons may be cited for this; one being the public schooling system and intimidation, but the medium of Internet radio provides a platform for rigorous debate and a flow of ideas, all within responsible boundaries, which a station code of conduct would determine.

Specialized radio is the new trend internationally and in the Palestinian media market, this concept would be unique, and with linkage to cell phones, the audience reach was anticipated to be wide and eventually it would grow internationally to lend a voice to the local youth globally. Most importantly, it did not require licensing and was not subject to any hostile interference both from the Palestinian Authority and Israel and the university provided it an element of credibility in the community.

On good faith, I got stuck into the project, but after a week Lucy informed me that they did not have funds to pay me. She drove a brand-new car, covered herself with designer accessories, had the latest Apple laptop, and she was busy constructing a video conferencing center at IMM, and they did not have money?

Nevertheless, I was so keen to get my idea off the ground that I even suggested that I use my own contacts with the Americans and others to obtain funds. She even feigned ignorance when I mentioned key persons whom I knew, only to learn later that they were in fact friends of hers too. Anyway, in my naivety and search for funds, I learned that she had a reputation of being corrupt and I was advised by Palestinians in the know, to extricate myself, which I then did.

Later, I learned that she went ahead with my idea, but launched the Internet radio station from Jerusalem and the Israelis shut it down on launch, for which she then sought donor sympathy and additional funds.

In short, victims and victimhood in the context of Western and Arab guilt has become a fine art by those who come up with ingenious ideas and projects to provide band aid solutions that merely exacerbate the problem, is what I learned from this experience.

Just as I was getting despondent, I received a call from the Center for Continuing Education in Ramallah (CCE) and learned that they were putting together a European Union funded project, led by Grenoble University in France, and in collaboration with universities in Jordan, Morocco, Lebanon and Greece—a Mediterranean initiative. The person who had partially designed a course in intercultural communication dropped out and they now sought my expertise.

After my previous disappointment with Ghassan, I was somewhat wary, but nevertheless I opted to see them to determine what it was they needed. I was then scheduled to meet the head of the project at the CCE to discuss my envisaged role and negotiated remuneration. I arrived early, as always, and was made to wait in the office of the manager. As I was engrossed deep in thought, whether this would be another disappointment or not, in walked a pretty girl with beautiful green eyes and a huge smile that lit up her lovely face, she said, "I am Miss Lama, pleased to meet you."

I was bowled over. Expecting a matronly looking woman or maybe a nerdy academic. She was indeed a sight for sore eyes. Later, she admitted that she too expected, after reading what she called my impressive CV, an "old ambassador-type."

After the usual pleasantries she got down to business, explaining the entire project to me and how, after the person who began with the intercultural communication course dropped out, they then found me through contacts who suggested that I would be the appropriate person.

Lama was forthright, "I am managing the project, but I shall put you in direct contact with professor Harald Herring at Grenoble university, who heads this particular course and he will guide you along."

This seemed fair and then we had to discuss my remuneration, and I was in for another pleasant revelation. Lama was so transparent which I was surprised with, especially after my previous bad experiences. She showed me the ballpark figures that she could negotiate around and indicated that she would pay me the maximum, although she believed with my qualifications and experience, I deserved much more. And furthermore, I would be paid separately for the curriculum and course notes.

All this, was so refreshing, especially her honesty, a rare commodity in the prison of occupation, that is Palestine. By this time, I had surmised that Palestine is a huge, open-air prison and the incarceration of the prisoners within had brought out the worst in them.

Lama and I agreed on the terms. She then walked me to the door. She was a petite woman with a huge personality and kindness but, I soon figured out, she also possessed a steely determination and resolve to succeed. In short, she was committed, passionate and a stickler for attention to details, all the hallmarks of me and my successes to date. I later learned that she came from the city of Jenin in the north, studied English literature at Birzeit University and then completed her master's in public administration in Germany, after doing a working stint in the private sector.

That evening I contacted Harald who, with his German background, was also into perfection. The subject matter was his specialty and it was indeed a pleasure to work with a person of his caliber. Lama took a personal interest in the subject matter, and unlike the other subjects handled by a host of experts she assisted me in no small measure. It took months to research, obtain Harald's approval, and then formalize the curriculum and notes, with Lama assisting in the typing thereof.

I then traveled to meet my colleagues or fellow lecturers from Palestine and the other countries in Rabat, Morocco, where I also saw Harald for the first time. We spent a week discussing the entire program and how we would cooperate and coordinate activities via an Internet portal that Grenoble had set up. This was the beginning of E-learning and I was privileged to be on board.

On my return, I began my thirty-hour program with twenty-five post-graduates from the Palestinian IT Sector over a period of 10 Saturday mornings. My approach was different and very interactive. I would spend the beginning of each session reviewing the last session's work with the assignment given to the class, then the next hour presenting new material and wrapping up the session with an interactive discussion. This enabled my students to internalize the lessons which were further cemented by my stories related to concepts that made it, not only easier to grasp, but to remember for a long time to come.

In the end, each student had to present a project and I must add that the enthusiasm that the class manifested was noted by all at the CCE. At the end they all, in their feedback, applauded what I had not only taught them but how I had inspired them and made life changing differences for many of them.

But after completing my work, I had to literally beg for payment and after having been given the run around and issuing many threats of my own, I was finally paid out. I learned from Lama that her principals were not interested in education but instead used the vehicle of education to travel, have fun and make money. Like I said before, it was all about prisoners, prison and temporary respite.

Anyway, with the experience of having designed and implemented a course, which in our globalized world is the key to success today, I was not only enriched but believed it was time to move to pastures anew, and they beckoned once more.

By chance, I bumped into an acquaintance working for the US Consulate General in Jerusalem. I learned that they were about to have a team building exercise at the Intercontinental hotel in Jericho and were busy considering proposals from various trainers. She learned what I was doing and suggested that I go along and make a pitch, which I did and successfully obtained the assignment.

Regular team building exercises revolved around fun and games but my approach was very different, built on material I obtained from my days at the Leadership Institute in Pretoria.

I dealt with Americans and Palestinians and succeeded in bringing them together, receiving much acclaim from all, with the American diplomats even saying, "Why didn't the State Department teach us this?" and with the Palestinians earnestly requesting copies of my notes. Basically, my South African notes from the Leadership Institute in Pretoria was the basis of this workshop.

Following on this success, I got involved with Amideast, an American funded NGO and trained a group of young Palestinian diplomats on communication, protocol and diplomacy, which I really enjoyed. However, I learned that although some of my students had already obtained their masters degrees whilst others were embarking on theirs, overseas postings depended primarily on Fatah party affiliation and meritocracy, like in South Africa, had taken a back seat. Sad indeed, as some of them had the potential to make a marked difference on the international stage.

Hot on the heels of this training, I worked with a group of Palestinians from the World Food Program and then a group from the Central Elections Commission, all at Amideast. Making a difference to people's lives by providing them with skills and tools as well as inspiring them, was very rewarding for me.

And then through my good friend, Dr Sabri Saidam, the minister of telecommunications who gave us the RAM FM license and who went onto become IT Advisor to the President, I regularly lectured to MBA students at Birzeit University on topics ranging from communications, presentations, creative thinking and conflict management, changing the concept of lecturing by telling stories and creating interactive discussions.

All in all, I was making a discernible difference to people's lives and money mattered not; it was just another calling that I willingly responded to, but I still yearned for radio.

8 Radio Nissa FM

A pioneering women radio station in the Arab world

AND THEN FROM NOWHERE, a Swiss philanthropist appeared. Yann Borgstad is involved in women empowerment projects across the world—a school for girls in Afghanistan, a job-creation project for women in Morocco and in Palestine, university scholarships for women. He believes women empowerment benefits the entire society. On meeting Maysoun in a restaurant in East Jerusalem, he floated the idea of a women radio station in Palestine. Yann was informed by various Palestinian friends that Maysoun was just the person who could do it for him.

Upon learning about this novel idea, I reminded Maysoun, "Rikki Kitaro the Israeli psychic once said, after RAM FM, you would open an Arabic radio station."

Maysoun's first reaction to Yann's idea was, "No!" She was not keen on another radio station and most of her friends were extremely skeptical.

I then reminded her of what Nelson Mandela said, "Freedom cannot be achieved unless women have been emancipated from all forms of oppression . . . Our endeavors must be about the liberation of the woman, the emancipation of the man and the liberty of the child."

A discussion followed on South Africa's journey from apartheid. Apartheid in South Africa was repugnant to Blacks. Yet it also discriminated against women. Since 1994 in South Africa, women have been taking their rightful place in all echelons of business, politics, and society. Most importantly we should be inspired by it.

After giving much thought to Yann's idea and playing devil's advocate, we realized there was merit in the idea. We did believe that Palestinian freedom had to be underpinned with women rights.

I then assisted Maysoun in writing the concept paper and creating a detailed business plan that included all the technical details. Unlike Issie's *modus operandi,* Yann sought detail. He especially wanted to see the numbers. He was a bottom-line guy. After the lessons we learned from the experience of setting up RAM FM and rising from its ashes, we proposed a lean, mean, and focused operation that would not only keep costs down but also would be productive, with both high quality and high volume. Let's say wisdom comes with time and experience. In this case, we had to thank RAM FM.

Yann approved the concept paper and business plan, then committed to provide the seed capital for the radio station.

Once again, it was the same run-around through various ministries to seek approval and licenses. However, after the closure of RAM FM by the Israelis, with Maysoun's short prison episode, she had obtained credibility among Palestinians. This helped somewhat to ease the journey.

I tagged along. When Maysoun encountered corrupt or chauvinistic individuals in the bureaucracy, I used my former status as diplomat with credentials to keep the project moving.

We rented a small two-room office, set up an Internet radio station and recruited staff, whom I began to instruct. It was different for me this time around, as I now trained. I was able to pass on institutional radio knowledge and experience in English. The station was going to be in Arabic, but the techniques and principles remained the same.

Concurrently, we ordered a transmitter from Tony, an Arab-Israeli based in the north, who fronted for his Jewish-Israeli partner. They were Sergey's only competitor.

Thereafter we began to set-up the technical equipment in another building and to construct the studios and offices. Coming on board was Mohamed, a former RAM FM technical guy, with loads of experience under his belt and in a short time we had a studio, offices, and transmitter with a signal beaming. In less than three months, we were ready for launch.

I spent many weeks training the Breakfast Show host, Nisreen and the Drive Show host, Hala, on all aspects of presenting and operating their respective programs. We opted to begin with just two shows and fill in the others as we went along.

My part of the work was to design the form or packaging according to international standards while adapting it for the station's unique needs. Maysoun's part was to create unique content that would bring in listeners.

Launch day arrived and Yann flew in from Geneva. I met him for the first time. He was young, energetic, highly motivated. He had an entrepreneurial flair and worked with intensity. Together with Maysoun they launched Nissa FM on 20 June 2010, at the same venue in Ramallah, where RAM FM was launched.

The interest was high: locally, regionally and internationally. It was the first women radio station in the Arab world and of all places, in Ramallah, Palestine.

Yann was beaming, the project did not take long to be on air and it did not cost much, we kept the costs to the bare minimum. Unlike RAM FM, this was not a commercial radio, but a not-for-profit entity, meaning whatever profits accrued, they would go back into women related social projects.

Yann provided the start-up costs and the running costs for the first two years of operation and then the station had to sustain itself with commercials and grants for programs from international organizations.

As for the philosophy of a woman radio station, Maysoun made it very clear from the onset, "We are not a feminist radio station and we are not anti-men. In fact, in demanding equality for women, we have to accept men as equal partners."

Yann Borgstadt

Local radio was generally very unprofessional, and Radio Nissa FM was like a breath of fresh air, with its quality programming and superb presenters, with many Palestinians even perceiving it to be a regional radio station. Listeners grew rapidly in number and men became hooked as well, which the initial surveys and findings surprised us with.

In essence, Nissa FM set out to build bridges between men and women, like RAM FM did between warring Semitic cousins.

Besides training the women presenters, my role was also to set-up the programming clocks and create the general style guide of the station. The station was called Radio Nissa FM, Nissa an Arabic word meaning women. The goal was to entertain with music, to inform with news, to educate with talk shows by hosting experts in various fields, and most importantly to inspire and empower women of Palestine. They make up more than half the society and graduate in larger numbers than men, but are then not represented accordingly in the workforce.

On the day of the launch, I sat in the studio to assist both Nisreen and Hala but then extricated myself the day after, leaving them on their own— another first for local radio.

Radio in Palestine generally employs one person to do the presenting, another to operate the panel and one more to place the calls. With so many drivers involved the car, or show, loses direction. To explain this, Nisreen the breakfast show presenter, would come in the morning and do her show all on her own, playing the music, producing her show, placing listeners on air and she would proudly say, "I am a one woman show!"

That was my humble contribution to women empowerment in radio!

More about Nisreen—she came from the Palestinian refugee camp of

Kalandia; her family having been displaced from the Jerusalem area. She was a passionate student, made great progress and grew with confidence. She was so empowered that she even purchased a small car and drove to and from the studio. Nisreen soon obtained recognition for her talents, especially her interviewing skills, based on research and arduous work. European media outlets, on Maysoun's recommendation, invited her to France and Denmark and that followed with a US consulate-sponsored trip to learn about radio during the election campaign that saw Barack Obama re-elected. On her return she excitedly informed me, "Raf, I was at a university in Chicago and a female student came up to me and told me that she listens to me every morning on the Internet." That spoke volumes about the reach of Nissa FM and Nisreen's popularity.

Like RAM FM, Nissa FM created much media hype and until today, the story continues as it grows and rides on wave after wave of success. For me, it was not only nice to see Maysoun back where she belonged and achieving, but in continuing to support her in her mission of informing, inspiring and empowering her sisters, it added a new dimension to my own life, the husband standing behind a successful woman, changing stereotypes in a male-dominated society, and by being a former South African ambassador, even enhancing it.

Unlike RAM FM, commercials began to come in fast and furious and the station began to make money and expand. Maysoun was soon feted with international recognition in terms of many social entrepreneurship awards—Schwab Fellowship (World Economic Forum), The Clinton Global Initiative Award, Ashoka Fellowship, Synergos Fellowship and then the equivalent of a knighthood by Palestinian President Mahmoud Abbas, the Cavalier Award.

Obama was the first US President to appoint an ambassador for women's affairs, and Ambassador Melanne Verveer honored Nissa FM with her presence, with Maysoun even interviewing her and translating her comments into Arabic. Hollywood actress Rosanna Arquette followed, and many Canadians and Americans have graced Nissa FM, including ministers, governors and senators. Such is the interest in this pioneering woman social empowerment radio project.

Once my initial work in training the presenters and launching the station was complete, I stepped back, but continued to monitor and assist whenever the need arose. After all, it is an all-women radio station.

Later, in December 2012, I was recalled by Yann as a consultant to do a detailed assessment and advice on a marketing and sales strategy to take Nissa FM forward.

I used a restaurant analogy to explain the workings of a radio station.

In a restaurant, the kitchen is the heart, and in a radio station it is the transmitter, antennae systems and broadcasting equipment. If the kitchen equipment has shortcomings, the food that is dished out, regardless of the decor, the cooks, menu, service, and marketing, paying customers will go elsewhere. Likewise, with a radio station, having the best music, presenters, programs and marketing and sales strategy means absolutely nothing if the signal that is transmitted has shortcomings, listeners will move to other stations. Simply, great food sells itself and great music and programming likewise sells itself. But then it's all about the cooking!

My assessment began with a thorough audit of the kitchen, meaning the transmitters, antennae systems, transmission and studio broadcast equipment. Later, I progressed to assess the menus, the cooks and the food, meaning the programming or product the radio station dishes out, all of which impact on the marketing and sales strategy.

Like RAM FM, Nissa FM also faced signal interference and transmission coverage issues.

Once more, I ascertained, Palestine is under occupation and the Israelis control everything from human movement to the air waves. The reality is that the FM frequency is in a total mess. International practice is to allocate space between frequencies for radio stations to minimize interference and furthermore to guarantee clarity, radio transmitters include filters. This does not happen in Palestine, as we also learned with RAM FM.

Then, the topography of the region adversely affects the FM transmission. To aggravate matters, the territory is so small that radio stations from Jordan, Syria and Lebanon reach here as well.

The devised solution to this problem was to acquire additional frequencies and focus transmission on specific regions, as distance opens a signal to interference, which localized strength apparently counters. So, Nissa FM took this route and today it has three frequencies 96 FM (Ramallah), 92.2 FM (Hebron), 96.2 FM (Nablus) directed at the North, Central and South of the West Bank, with the latter directed towards the Gaza Strip.

Nissa FM also faced this challenge: does it change its menu/presentation to feed the needs of the masses to obtain a larger listener base, at the expense of its women focus and quality of presentation or not? The aspect of women is what the station's social message is based on, otherwise Nissa FM simply becomes just another of the myriad of radio stations in Palestine. Nissa FM has a unique identity and the branding is based on its quality and professionalism, which leading media personalities in Palestine have already acknowledged. So Nissa FM continues doing what it began, for this radio station it is not about the numbers. It is about the quality rather than quantity and its primary goal is the impact it makes on women's lives.

I then recommended setting up a newsroom with two women reporters, one for the morning shift and one for the afternoon, obtain news items from Nissa FM's community reporters in the West Bank and Gaza, pen the news, take feeds from international TV like Al Jazeera and, on the hour, walk into the studio to read quality news bulletins designed on international best practice of concentric circles, in the order of local, regional and international news. With these two professionally trained newswomen, Nissa FM can even have breaking news bulletins and down the line, Nissa FM may consider syndicating and selling news feeds to regional and international radio.

This was immediately implemented with the appointment of two women news reporters. I then involved myself in training them in all aspects of news reporting and set-up a dedicated newsroom, transforming the meeting room, which used to be my office in the past and which gave me an objective view of the station.

The audience is the key component of a radio station. Without an audience the entire rationale for the station's existence is questionable. Going back to the restaurant analogy, the audience may be likened to the paying customers without whom the restaurant ceases to exist. Local surveys conducted by reputable pollsters indicated phenomenal listener growth and this helped in increasing commercial traffic as well as obtaining grants from international organizations.

The difference between a restaurant and a radio station can be summed up as follows: the former serves food whereas the latter serves food for thought and entertainment. Marketing differs in that one seeks to get people to eat, whereas the other seeks to get people to listen. Most importantly, the major difference is in how revenues are obtained. Restaurants accrue revenue from paying customers whilst radio sells airtime to customers who advertise their products and services to listeners whom they have captivated with programming.

Cognizance was taken of the Palestinian media environment which is truly unique, in that unlike many nations, including much of the Arab world; it suffers from an overabundance of media outlets. In addition, the legal environment is affected by a media law that is at odds with the basic law and a press and publications law that is being reworked. On the last count, there were thirty television stations, forty-five radio stations and four newspapers. This media saturation for a total population of about four million is the consequence of the Palestinian Authority's decision, early in the negotiations during the Oslo process, to ensure the setting up of as many de facto stations as possible, to strengthen its negotiating position.

Thus, the substantial number of stations has resulted in a limited economic base for broadcasters. The population size and the Palestinian economy does not support sufficient advertising revenues, and contributing to it is a lack of professionalism in journalism.

Palestine's economy is totally dependent on donors and aid monies, all subject to the dictates of the Israeli occupation. No figures are available for yearly advertising budgets and what percentage is allocated to radio.

With limited resources and women power, Nissa FM's unique selling proposition (USP) is a focused and professionally operated radio station, targeting a segment of society that makes informed decisions on consumer products and services, and thus the target market has been defined and accordingly addressed in programming for growth. Nissa FM informs potential advertisers about its platform and the benefits it offers their products/services. An additional selling strategy has been to include interviews with advertisers (airtime for PR), as part of a package deal.

Nissa FM's edge is that it positions potential advertisers' products in a focused manner to a defined segment of society that generally spends the monies, unlike the competition which is generalized and takes a shotgun approach.

All in all, Nissa's programming was developed with the consumer in mind, the advertisers' needs as a primary concern (it is a commercial radio station), but most of all, the station's appeal is structured on life changing experiences for its listeners.

I then recommended, learning from the successful experience of Primedia in Johannesburg, an outside broadcast vehicle which Nissa FM should seek funds/donations for, probably in Europe and equip it to roam the West Bank on weekends to do live shows. Take the station to the people!

This materialized with the Swiss Representative Office in Ramallah donating a small vehicle.

Proposals for grants and other sources of income for capital expenditure and growth should be continually researched and applied for, both locally and by the principals in Geneva. And this now continues to happen with growing success.

My work was done, and it was time for me to finally extricate myself from Nissa FM and for Maysoun to take total control and drive it into unexplored territory by creating a Nissa Network in partnership with regional radio stations.

Still wanting to recreate RAM FM, it was during the early days of Nissa FM,

Raf with Team Nissa FM

we learned that a European organization, Hirondelle sought a consultant to set-up a radio station in Bethlehem. They had budgeted 50,000 euros for it, which was rather extravagant, having done it for so much less.

I then wondered if another RAM FM was in the offing in the holy city of Bethlehem!

Together with the technical staff of Radio Nissa, we put together and submitted a detailed proposal, sure that with our track record of success with two radio stations, we would win it.

But it was not to be. A local polling company, Near East Consulting won it. At the end, they presented a poll, that was laughable, about the state of radio in Palestine and no radio station was ever set up, though they pocketed 50,000 euros.

Later in the year, Maysoun met some of the staff from Hirondelle in Europe and they admitted that they were conned out of 50,000 euros—victims and con-artists abound in the Holy Land.

As I continued to use the meeting room at the offices of Nissa FM to write, it was there that I was visited by my friend Mohammed, who went on to complete his masters in Conflict Resolution and Mitigation studies at Tel Aviv University. He brought along his American professor, Brian Polkinghorn and wife, Lucy and his Israeli-American colleagues Adam and Joe. They came to see me to talk about RAM FM and the role it played. Brian was the program director at the Conflict Analysis and Dispute Resolution Center, Salisbury

University in America as well as a Fulbright Ambassador. He was also doing a stint at Tel Aviv University.

I enjoyed engaging with them in a very meaningful discussion and even added that only after the closure of RAM FM we realized the positive role we had played and how everyone missed us. Nevertheless, it was time to move on and Nissa FM was the next stage in the evolution of our radio journey.

In passing, I mentioned to Brian that I was seized on completing a collection of short stories, related to my life and he expressed an interest in reading them. I obliged by sending them to him by email that afternoon.

Brian's response bowled me over:

> This is the story of a crafty thinker, a highly intelligent book smart dude who also has—in a rare combination I might add—street smarts. Wooo! What a combination—and look at the journey! Inspirational? Yes! Funny? Yes! Contemplative? Yes!
>
> The book is a magnum opus for the common man who can connect to you on many levels. I do hope you continue to write and build a growing audience (fan base!) that will laugh as hard as I did and fall prey to deep dark emotions that surface when the cranky old farts who seem to know what is right with the social order get in the way of our happiness.

And it wasn't long before Brian contacted me and wondered if I would travel to his university to talk on his international guest program, "One Person Can Make a Difference" series. I immediately jumped at the opportunity, as he indicated that they would pay all travel and accommodation costs.

Thereafter, we discussed the topic and the angle I would take. We decided that I should say, "One person can make a difference by bending the rules." This would be my comment on my life's journey.

I hadn't been back to the United States since 1996 and I looked forward to the trip. Brian assisted with all the arrangements and after I obtained my visa and ticket I was on my way to Philadelphia and then on to Salisbury. Landing in Salisbury, reminded me of my days as a diplomat, landing at small airports on the west coast and working the local towns. It all felt like I was there before. Brian met me at the arrivals area, and it was nice to see a friend, with whom I related to for some time through the written word and we had time to then catch up via the spoken word. Let's say, we got along like the proverbial house on fire.

The university was pretty and at the onset of autumn in November 2013, it was a joy to be taken on a tour and Brian made it a point to walk into lectures and get me to virtually market my talk that night. Hey, this was the USA and marketing is the name of the game.

That evening the venue was packed and I did a two and half hour talk with a power point presentation. The first part was based on my early life through apartheid, diplomacy and the second part focused on RAM FM, with lots of musical clips that the audience really enjoyed. The question and answer period was loads of fun. I was truly humbled, when I learned that I had shared this venue with many notable international personalities, like Dr Arun Gandhi, the grandson of Gandhi, Gerry Adams from the IRA, De Klerk, the last South African White president and Desmond Tutu.

On my return, I met Dave Harden from USAID, who interviewed Maysoun and myself on the night of the launch of RAM FM at the American Colony hotel in Jerusalem. Dave had moved up to head the USAID office. "Raf, nice to see you. I miss RAM FM. Why don't you set it up again? We can help you. Contact my office; we have a program that deals with that sort of thing."

We exchanged cards and I contacted Brian Polkinghorn, my friends Adam Abrahams and Mohamed Ismail. Within the week, Adam and I traveled to Tel Aviv to meet with the USAID officers tasked with the program Dave spoke about, to obtain details and determine how to pitch our proposal.

Obtaining a radio license from the Israeli side was a non-starter with the right-wing government, and a Palestinian licensed station had many pitfalls.

I recommended that we go for an Internet radio station, based in Jerusalem. This was workable. But then we learned about the loads of paperwork required by USAID, we would be writing reports, assessments and doing impact studies etc. and have no time at all in airing a radio station, something none of us were keen to do.

Recalling my days at the SABC at Radio Lotus in Durban and the paperwork we did for every show. I once said on air, and for which I was severely reprimanded by my boss, "If archaeologists dig up this place, they will say this was a paper making factory and music was played to relieve the workers from the boredom of their work." And I certainly did not want to go down that route, with an Internet-based RAM FM, that called for more thumb suck paperwork than broadcasting. I finally dropped the idea of ever resuscitating RAM FM in any form whatsoever. That was it!

And then, from out of nowhere, the RAM FM case reared its head, surfacing after all these years, with Maysoun formally charged for operating an illegal radio station. We had believed that Issie's lawyer in Tel Aviv, Cookie, had settled the matter but it was not so. He simply washed his hands of it and left Maysoun to take the rap.

We secured the services of Shlomo Lekker, a human rights lawyer based in Jerusalem and a good friend, who then made Cookie and Issie aware that they were the shareholders and Maysoun was simply an employee and he hinted that they would have to answer, and it was not fair for Maysoun to take the rap alone.

Initially Shlomo indicated that he would cut a plea deal for Maysoun to do community service, like working in the Jerusalem zoo for a period. I thought it was surreal as the RAM FM studio used to be close by, was it also some kind of poetic justice. Maysoun was terrified of the prospect, as I chuckled.

On the day of the hearing, Maysoun and I headed to the court near the Russian compound where Maysoun had spent a night in custody. The proximity of the court to her place of incarceration added another scary dimension, but we had confidence in our friend Shlomo.

It was strange, sitting in court watching Shlomo arguing in Hebrew, with us watching the judge and his body language to try to figure out if he was going to rule in our favor or not.

Shlomo presented a very good case and settled for RAM FM paying a small fine, and the matter was closed for good. I admired my friend Shlomo's legal style, which was to settle matters rather than win battles and lose wars. "This is Israel and it is the only way" is what he said.

Issie eventually paid the fine and for Shlomo's services. We were then instructed by the Talpiot police to pick up the confiscated equipment which was totally damaged and useless, and going there brought back vivid memories.

The RAM FM case finally ended.

Nissa FM continues, ten years later, to build bridges between Palestinian men and women who comprise the unbreakable thread that holds together the quilt of society: empowering, inspiring and changing the lives of the latter for the better.

Today Nissa FM ranks number four amongst long established Palestinian radio stations. It is the first specialized station that offers an innovative concept to radio in Palestine, it is not only a broadcasting medium, it is also an empowerment medium. Nissa FM has grown from a core staff of four to fourteen and increased weekly programming to cover the entire day. It has trained over one-hundred women from across all spectrums of society on how to effectively use media. The station has interviewed over five-hundred Palestinian women in the diaspora and covered thousands of women success stories and most importantly it is changing the lives of Palestinian women.

Inspired by its success, it is not stopping, determined to move beyond its borders and across the region, Nissa FM plans to expand its model through the Nissa Network—which will include regional radio stations. The intent is through the network to expand this impact and social change to include Arab sisters in the region.

Maysoun says, "Previously, women had a glass ceiling imposed on them, limiting them to how high they could rise. But information and knowledge is the hammer that has shattered that ceiling. Knowledge and information that radio disseminates can never hamper women or chain us down. It gives us wings, unlocks new doors of opportunities and lets us form educated opinions. Make no mistake, only women themselves can determine how far they rise in life. And we at Nissa FM make every effort to show them that there are no limits!"

I continue living in exile in Jerusalem, as the ONLY South African married to a Palestinian. Watching from afar how South Africans, led by the African National Congress (ANC) of the late Nelson Mandela, have squandered our hard fought for freedom and replaced it with corruption that has led the beloved country into a quagmire, whilst Semitic cousins in the Holy Land of eternal conflict continue their struggle to find the ties that bind and hopefully live together peacefully.

Mainstream and alternative media in South Africa daily exposes the corruption that has eaten into the body politic of the rainbow nation, and I like many others have simply become numb.

In Israel, alternative media provides a platform for right to left narratives to be heard, but controls citing security and antisemitism continue to rule.

The same applies to Palestine, with fake news becoming the new boogie word, and security trumping it all.

In the end, RAM FM was way ahead of its time and Nissa FM is now playing a positive and meaningful role in women empowerment, built on the lessons of the former.

9 Epilogue

5th Annual Global Cyber-Conference on Dispute Resolution: Inter-Cultural Conflict, hosted by University of Alaska on April 15, 2015.

I was invited to be the keynote speaker and from my laptop, late at night, I spoke as follows:

> I am both honored and humbled to be able to join you from the land of eternal conflict, from the time of the Romans, to the Crusaders, the Turks, the British, and the Jordanians . . . the conflict continues . . . today the protagonists are Israelis and Palestinians.
>
> Ironically, whilst divisions widen and conflicts amongst humans on the terrestrial level continue, we are at the same time, reaching out and forging ties that bind, thanks to cyberspace!
>
> On the other hand, conflicts are so easy to resolve. Take the classic case of two kids fighting over the sharing of a cake. Who cuts the cake and who chooses? That is the question! To manage this with a win-win outcome . . . he that cuts the cake, lets the other choose.
>
> This places the onus on the first kid to make sure it is equally cut, and the conflict is then resolved to both kids' satisfaction.
>
> As a South African, who grew up during the worst days of apartheid, served as a diplomat during its last days and demise and then continued during the glorious Mandela years of peace and reconciliation. Today, twenty-one years after freedom and democracy, I can say the solution to ending apartheid was in essence, all players in the conflict, which was about color, race and culture, sat around a table, spoke to one another, and then jointly wrote a constitution. And the constitution addressed everyone's hopes and fears. Following that we had a democratic election and many more have followed since.
>
> I quote Nelson Mandela. "If you want to make peace with your enemy, you have to work with your enemy, and then he becomes your partner."
>
> Coming back to the eternal conflict in the Holy Land . . . in 2003, as South Africa's ambassador to Palestine, I had a ring-side seat on the

Palestinian side of the conflict and perceived it from that perspective, and admittedly it was also clouded by my South African experience.

In 2008, I made the transition from being an Ambassador to become a DJ and the host of the *only* political talk show, on 93.6 RAM FM, a radio station that provided a platform for both Palestinians and Israelis in English.

I then entered the ring itself and, in a sense, became a referee to the conflict.

It was then time for me to suspend my own perceptions, engage Israeli society and understand its fears and problems, and to give a voice to Palestinian society to articulate its hopes and aspirations. All to have a comprehensive picture of the conflict and to be an objective facilitator to peaceful dialogue.

Hosting guests from both sides and talking about issues that divided as well as united them, I learned eventually that no one wants to hear the truth!

As Frantz Fanon aptly said:

> Sometimes people hold a core belief that is very strong. When they are presented with evidence that works against that belief, the new evidence cannot be accepted. It would create a feeling that is extremely uncomfortable, called cognitive dissonance. And because it is so important to protect the core belief, they will rationalize, ignore and even deny anything that doesn't fit in with the core belief.

Today, as a detached observer, sitting far-away from the ring itself, I can say this conflict is all about land. One party believes they have a God-given title deed to the land, whereas the other believes it is their ancestral land.

After the 1st Intifada (uprising), managing of the conflict manifested in the Oslo Peace Accords which gave 78% of the Holy Land to Israel and 22% to Palestine.

Yet, it did not work!

Why?

Security became an issue for the Israelis.

Freedom remained the issue for the Palestinians.

This has dragged the conflict on and on . . . many consider it intractable!

Yet the solution is so simple . . . If one obtains freedom, the other gets security.

It's not for me to prescribe a solution, but I am of the firm conviction that if both sides sit down and seriously talk to address, fears, concerns and hopes, as we did in South Africa, it can be resolved.

It is the only way!

Otherwise the longer this conflict continues . . . the chances of obtaining a peaceful solution are fading away. . . . The alternative is fascism on one side and radicalism on the other—explosive ingredients for yet another bloody war!

All said and done, history has taught us many lessons that we generally continue to ignore:

Colonialism ushered in European superiority, but eventually came undone, beginning with the philosophy of Mahatma Gandhi, who began his journey in South Africa and played a key role in standing up against the British, obtaining India's freedom and democracy.

Hitler's Nazism, based on the notion of the superiority of the Aryan race, produced World War II and the holocaust that led to untold suffering and deaths of millions but was eventually checked by the allied forces before that cancer spread.

Stalin's Communism came up against western capitalism, which then led to a protracted cold war, eventually caving in to freedom and economic enslavement just like the rest.

Apartheid, conjured up by white Afrikaner nationalists, caused much grief and harm to millions who suffered under the yoke of an inhumane social system, eventually Nelson Mandela led the country from that abyss into an era of freedom and reconciliation. Sadly . . . today xenophobia has filled the vacuum left by apartheid and Africans are fighting/killing fellow Africans.

Zionism, based on the notion of the biblical "chosen people," has produced two *intifadas* (uprisings) and an intractable conflict in the Holy Land between Semitic cousins, with untold pain and suffering that has no end in sight.

Barrier Wall

American Exceptionalism, overt since 9/11 has produced a war on terror with no clear end point that has killed, maimed, or displaced millions of innocent people in the lands that house these elusive terrorists.

Colonialism, Nazism, Communism, Apartheid, Zionism and Exceptionalism all have the same root: one race or people believe . . . they are superior to the other.

It is this obsession with *us* and *them* that has led all of us into the abyss.

Human beings continue to divide on these unnatural notions and little do we realize that we are in fact sowing the seeds of our own destruction.

My own struggle and life's journey has taught me that until this

philosophy of one race being superior to another is thrown into the trashcan of history and we embrace our fellow humans as brothers and sisters in this common terrestrial journey . . . pain, suffering and wars shall continue.

To conclude, I would like to quote from "Two Suns in the Sunset," a Pink Floyd song:

> Ashes and diamonds
> Foe and friend
> We were all equal, in the end.

Acknowledgements

Thank you, Issie Kirsh, your vision of a radio station for Palestinians and Israelis, in a neutral language and unyielding commitment to realize it, led to this incredible initiative that translated into a memorable adventure.

Appreciation to the RAM FM team who came from far and wide, joined hands, and then took this amazing journey—you added color and meaning to the canvas of my life's experiences.

Kind words to US Consulate, USAID and EU, who were ready to provide a lifeline of rescue at the end of RAM FM.

Acknowledgment to Professor Brian Polkinghorn (Department of Conflict Analysis and Dispute Resolution at Salisbury University, and Fulbright Ambassador), who had the kindest words to say on reading my manuscript, which then motivated me to seek a publisher.

Thank you, Yann Borgstedt, your vision and determination to change the lives of women which you so passionately continue to do, led to another incredible radio initiative, which then gave me the opportunity to make a difference once more.

Heartfelt appreciation to Cune Press. Scott and his team guided me meticulously through the processes and made insightful suggestions in the development of this book.

A big thank you to my wife Maysoun and our son Adam, for your love and support through testing times in the Holy Land. Without you I would never have written this book.

Most important, appreciation to my Creator, for guiding me on this awesome journey, and continuing to do so.

About Cune Press

Cune Press was founded in 1994 to publish thoughtful writing of public importance. Our name is derived from "cuneiform." (In Latin cuni means "wedge.")

In the ancient Near East the development of cuneiform script—simpler and more adaptable than hieroglyphics—enabled a large class of merchants and landowners to become literate. Clay tablets inscribed with wedge-shaped stylus marks made possible a broad intermeshing of individual efforts in trade and commerce.

Cuneiform enabled scholarship to exist and art to flower, and created what historians define as the world's first civilization. When the Phoenicians developed their sound-based alphabet, they expressed it in cuneiform.

The idea of Cune Press is the democratization of learning, the faith that rarefied ideas, pulled from dusty pedestals and displayed in the streets, can transform the lives of ordinary people. And it is the conviction that ordinary people, trusted with the most precious gifts of civilization, will give our culture elasticity and depth—a necessity if we are to survive in a time of rapid change.

Books from Cune Press

Aswat: Voices from a Small Planet (a series from Cune Press)

Looking Both Ways	Pauline Kaldas
Stage Warriors	Sarah Imes Borden
Stories My Father Told Me	Helen Zughaib & Elia Zughaib
Girl Fighters	Carolyn Han

Syria Crossroads (a series from Cune Press)

Leaving Syria	Bill Dienst & Madi Williamson
Visit the Old City of Aleppo	Khaldoun Fansa
The Dusk Visito	Helen Zughaib, Elia Zughai
Steel & Silk	Sami Moubayed
Syria - A Decade of Lost Chances	Carsten Wieland
The Road from Damascus	Scott C. Davis
A Pen of Damascus Steel	Ali Ferzat
White Carnations	Musa Rahum Abbas

Bridge Between the Cultures (a series from Cune Press)

Empower a Refugee	Patricia Martin Holt
Biblical Time Out of Mind	Tom Gage, James A. Freeman
Afghanistan and Beyond	Linda Sartor
The Other Side of the Wall	Richard Hardigan
Apartheid Is a Crime	Mats Svensson
Curse of the Achille Lauro	Reem al-Nimer
Arab Boy Delivered	Paul A. Zarou

 Cune   Cune Press: www.cunepress.com

Rafique (Raf) Gangat grew up in Weenen, a small farming town in South Africa. A keen cricketer, in his youth he played for his province. He graduated from the University of KwaZulu-Natal in English & Philosophy. After university, he dabbled in the music industry and radio before becoming a diplomat. He was the first ever diplomat of color for South Africa. He represented South Africa in Beverly Hills (Vice-Consul), Head Office (Spokesperson), Karachi (Consul General), Abu Dhabi (Ambassador), Head-Office (North Africa Division), and finally Palestine (Ambassador).

After 2003, Raf worked to create a radio station modeled on Radio 702 in South Africa, an institution which Nelson Mandela judged had played a significant role in reconciliation in post-Apartheid /South Africa. In Palestine, Raf pursued his love of radio and popular music and launched an ambitious effort to marry diplomacy and media through community radio.

In 2012 he published *Ye Shall Bowl on Grass,* a memoir of his life during and after the South Africa apartheid era.

Raf now works as a communications and media consultant and lives in Jerusalem.

For more: www.rafiquegangat.com

CPSIA information can be obtained
at www.ICGtesting.com
Printed in the USA
JSHW020708150522
25717JS00002B/1

9 781951 082178